Poison Ivy and Poison Oak

This weed (above) gives you an itchy rash. Poison Ivy grows like a vine, and Poison Oak like a shrub. Try to remember what the leaves look like, and do not touch it. If you do touch it, washing your hands as soon as possible may reduce the itching. Your local drug store will also have various remedies.

Parts of an Insect

All insects have the following things in common:
1 An outside skeleton (or exo-skeleton)
2 Three pairs of jointed legs
3 A body divided into three sections: head, thorax, and abdomen
4 External mouthparts on their head

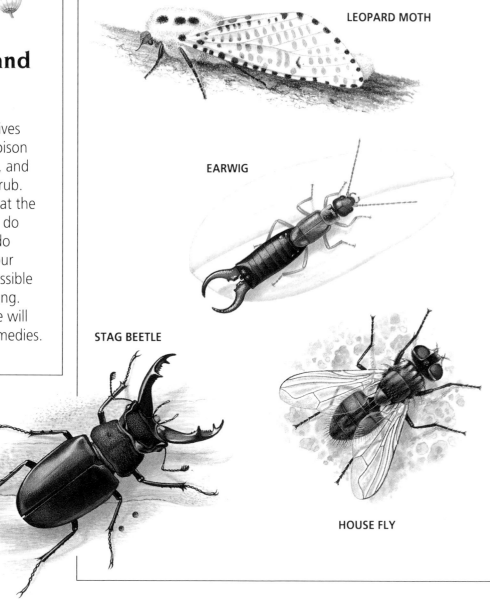

LEOPARD MOTH

EARWIG

STAG BEETLE

HOUSE FLY

SCIENCE NATURE GUIDES

INSECTS
OF NORTH AMERICA

Dr George C. McGavin

ILLUSTRATIONS BY
Richard Lewington

EDITED BY
Leslie Jackman

THUNDER BAY
P·R·E·S·S

Conservation

There are about 200,000 individual insects for every one human on the Earth. Most insects live in the tropics, and over half of them live in tropical rain forests. Many different insects also live in wetlands—like flood plains, marshes, and swamps.

Unfortunately these two habitats are the ones that are most at risk in the world today. People are felling the tropical rain forests for the hardwoods, like mahogany, to make furniture, or clearing them for farms. People are draining wetlands because they are good places to farm once the water has gone. Either way, unique insect species are being lost every day—some scientists estimate the planet is losing over a thousand species a year.

On page 78 you will find the names of some organizations who campaign for the protection of particular animals and habitats in America and around the world. By joining them and supporting their efforts, **you** can help to preserve our wildlife.

Insect Hunter's Code

1 **Always go collecting with a friend,** and always tell an adult where you have gone.
2 **Treat all insects with care**—most are delicate creatures and can be easily killed by rough handling.
3 **Leave insects' nests** untouched.
4 **Ask permission** before exploring or crossing private property.
5 **Keep to footpaths** as much as possible.
6 **Keep off crops and leave fence gates** as you find them.
7 **Wear long pants, shoes, and a long-sleeved shirt** in deer tick country.
8 **Ask your parents only to light fires** in a fireplace in special picnic areas.

Thunder Bay Press
5880 Oberlin Drive
Suite 400
San Diego, CA 92121

First published in the United States
by Thunder Bay Press, 1995

Simplified text and captions by Leslie Jackman, based on *Insects of the Northern Hemisphere* by George C. McGavin.

Species illustrations by Richard Lewington. Habitat paintings by Philip Weare of Lindon Artists. Headbands by Antonia Phillips. Identification and activities illustrations by Mr Gay Galsworthy.

Editor   Diana Briscoe
Designer   James Lawrence
Design Assistants   Victoria Furbisher
                    Karen Ferguson
Art Director   John Strange
Editorial Director Pippa Rubinstein

Library of Congress Cataloging in Publication Data
McGavin. George.
    Insects / George C. McGavin.
        p.   ca. — (Science Nature Guides)
    Includes bibliographical references (p.78) and index.
    ISBN 1–57145–017–3 : $12.95
    1. Insects—North America—Juvenile literature.
    2. Insects—North America—Identification—
        Juvenile literature. [1. Insects.]
I. Title   II. Series
QL473.M37   1995
595.7'097—dc20
                                        94–27459
                                            CIP
                                            AC

Printed in Italy

Contents

What Is an Insect?

There are over 1.5 million species of animals to be found on Earth, and nearly 932,000 of them are insects. Because there are so many different insects, this book deals only with families of insects, not with their separate species.

Insects are invertebrates, which means that they do not have an internal backbone as fish or snakes or dogs do. The first insects developed between 300 and 400 million years ago—long before the dinosaurs!

The success of many insects is partly because they can fly. With wings, insects can travel long distances to colonize new habitats and they can escape from their enemies. Some can beat their wings as often as 1,000 beats per second.

There are so many different families of insects, that you will have to observe very carefully. Keep looking until you have memorized every detail. By doing this you will discover how wonderfully insects are made.

From egg to insect

Insects are divided into groups, called Orders. The most advanced insect orders, like Coleoptera or Lepidoptera, have a very complicated life cycle during which they change their shape three times. Each time they look completely different from their previous shape. How this works is shown in the picture. The fly life cycle can be as short as 14 days; the adults will live several weeks.

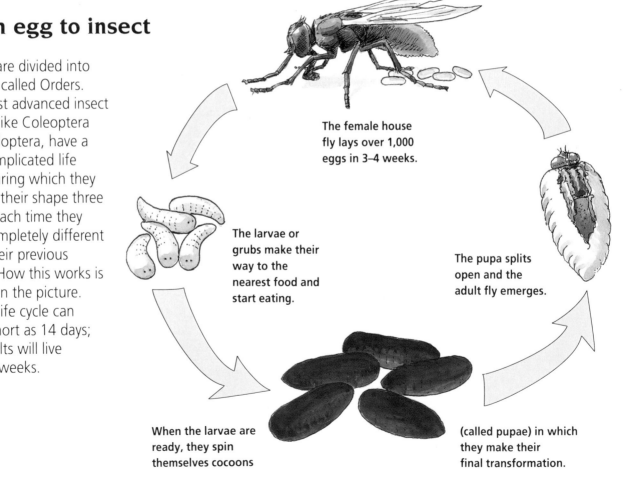

The female house fly lays over 1,000 eggs in 3–4 weeks.

The larvae or grubs make their way to the nearest food and start eating.

When the larvae are ready, they spin themselves cocoons

(called pupae) in which they make their final transformation.

The pupa splits open and the adult fly emerges.

Orders for insects

There are nearly 932,000 species of insects, sub-divided into smaller groups called Orders. There are more than twenty-five orders, but as over 1,000 new species of insects are described every year, this is constantly changing. These are the largest orders:

COLEOPTERA
Beetles
(about 370,000)

LEPIDOPTERA
Butterflies & Moths
(about 165,000)

HYMENOPTERA
Sawflies, Bees,
Wasps, & Ants
(about 120,000)

HEMIPTERA
Bugs, Hoppers,
& Aphids
(about 90,000)

ORTHOPTERA
Grasshoppers
& Crickets
(about 19,000)

DIPTERA
Flies
(about 119,500)

Habitat Picture Bands

This book is divided into different habitats (types of countryside). Each habitat has a different picture band at the top of the page. These are shown below.

Found Almost
Everywhere

Grasslands

Woods &
Forests

Deserts &
Savanna

Rivers, Bogs,
& Wetlands

Pests &
Parasites

How to use this book

This book will introduce you to the commoner families of insects. Each family has an entry and a picture of a typical insect from the family. When trying to identify the insect you have found, expect it to look something like the picture, but not exactly the same. To identify an insect, follow these steps.

1 **Look at the list of the commonest orders and their pictures** shown here. Which does it most resemble? The identification chart on pages 6–7 will help to narrow down the options.

2 **Decide what habitat you are in.** If you aren't sure, read the descriptions at the start of each section to see which one fits best. Each habitat has a different picture band heading and these are shown here.

3 **Look through the pages of insects with this picture band.** The picture and information given for each insect family will help you to identify it. The large winged insect (below) is a Hawk Moth (see page 23.)

4 **If you can't find the insect there,** look through the other sections. Some species of an insect family may live in a different habitat. Pests and parasites move with their hosts. You will find the small insect (below) is a Predaceous Diving Beetle (see page 63.)

5 **If you still can't find the insect,** you may have to look in a larger field guide (see page 79 for some suggestions.) You might have spotted something very rare or even unknown!

What Is It?

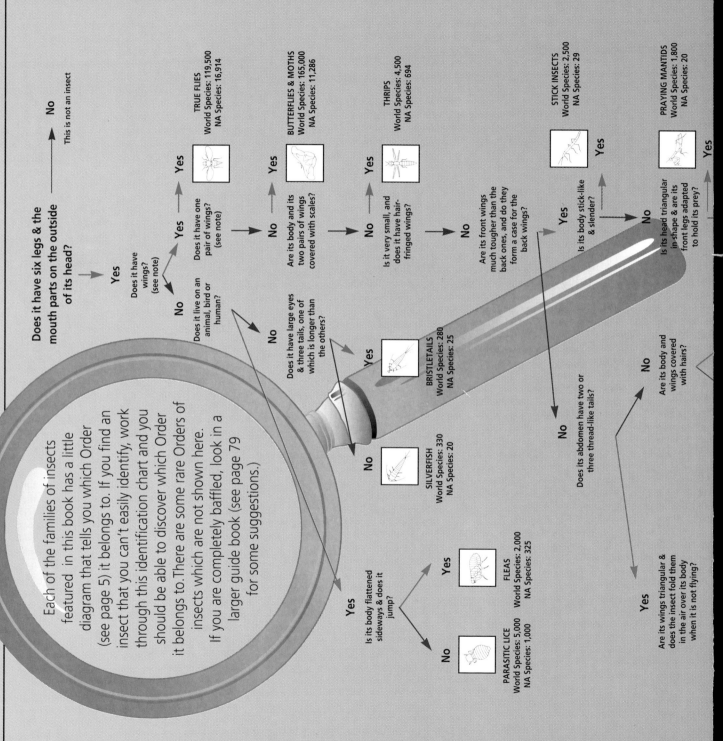

Does it have six legs & the mouth parts on the outside of its head?

No → This is not an insect

Yes ↓

Does it have wings? (see note)

Yes → Does it have one pair of wings? (see note)

Yes → **TRUE FLIES** World Species: 119,500 NA Species: 16,914

No → Are its body and its two pairs of wings covered with scales?

Yes → **BUTTERFLIES & MOTHS** World Species: 165,000 NA Species: 11,286

No → Is it very small, and does it have hair-fringed wings?

Yes → **THRIPS** World Species: 4,500 NA Species: 694

No → Are its front wings much tougher than the back ones, and do they form a case for the back wings?

Yes → Is its body stick-like & slender?

Yes → **STICK INSECTS** World Species: 2,500 NA Species: 29

No → Is its head triangular in-shape & are its front legs adapted to hold its prey?

Yes → **PRAYING MANTIDS** World Species: 1,800 NA Species: 20

No ↓

No → Does it live on an animal, bird or human?

Yes → Is its body flattened sideways & does it jump?

Yes → **FLEAS** World Species: 2,000 NA Species: 325

No → **PARASITIC LICE** World Species: 5,000 NA Species: 1,000

No → Does it have large eyes & three tails, one of which is longer than the others?

Yes → **BRISTLETAILS** World Species: 280 NA Species: 25

No → **SILVERFISH** World Species: 330 NA Species: 20

No → Does its abdomen have two or three thread-like tails?

No → Are its body and wings covered with hairs?

Yes → Are its wings triangular & does the insect fold them in the air over its body when it is not flying?

Each of the families of insects featured in this book has a little diagram that tells you which Order (see page 5) it belongs to. If you find an insect that you can't easily identify, work through this identification chart and you should be able to discover which Order it belongs to. There are some rare Orders of insects which are not shown here. If you are completely baffled, look in a larger guide book (see page 79 for some suggestions.)

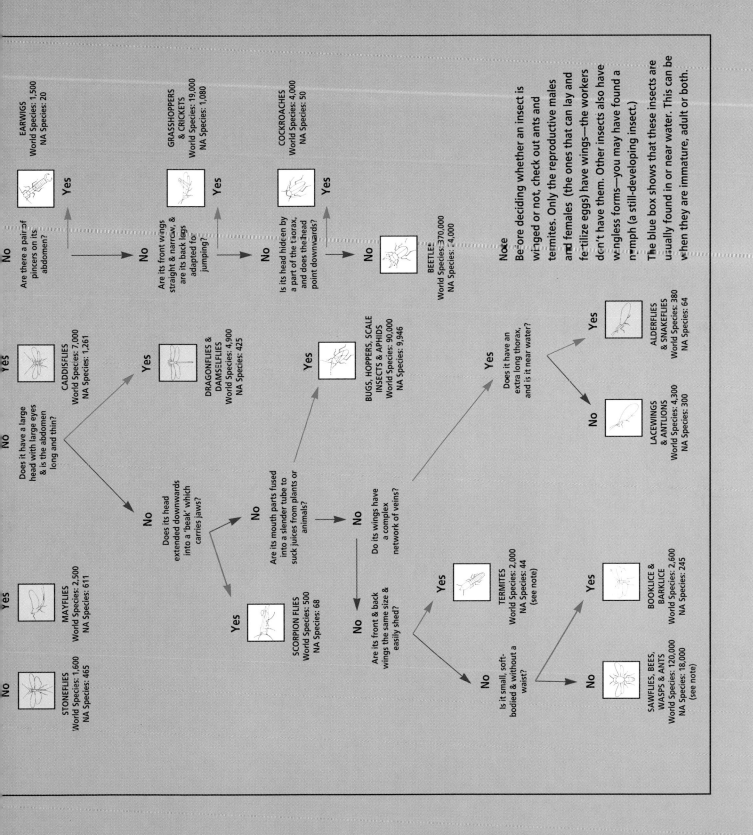

No — **Does it have a large head with large eyes & is the abdomen long and thin?** — **Yes**

No

STONEFLIES
World Species: 1,600
NA Species: 465

Yes

MAYFLIES
World Species: 2,500
NA Species: 611

Yes

CADDISFLIES
World Species: 7,000
NA Species: 1,261

No — **Does its head extended downwards into a 'beak' which carries jaws?**

Yes

DRAGONFLIES & DAMSELFLIES
World Species: 4,900
NA Species: 425

No — **Are its mouth parts fused into a slender tube to suck juices from plants or animals?**

Yes

SCORPION FLIES
World Species: 500
NA Species: 68

Yes

BUGS, HOPPERS, SCALE INSECTS & APHIDS
World Species: 90,000
NA Species: 9,946

No — **Do its wings have a complex network of veins?**

No — **Are its front & back wings the same size & easily shed?**

Yes

TERMITES
World Species: 2,000
NA Species: 44
(see note)

No — **Is it small, soft-bodied & without a waist?**

Yes

BOOKLICE & BARKLICE
World Species: 2,600
NA Species: 245

No

SAWFLIES, BEES, WASPS & ANTS
World Species: 120,000
NA Species: 18,000
(see note)

Yes — **Does it have an extra long thorax, and is it near water?**

Yes

ALDERFLIES & SNAKEFLIES
World Species: 380
NA Species: 64

No

LACEWINGS & ANTLIONS
World Species: 4,300
NA Species: 300

No — **Are there a pair of pincers on its abdomen?** — **Yes**

EARWIGS
World Species: 1,500
NA Species: 20

No — **Are its front wings straight & narrow, & are its back legs adapted for jumping?** — **Yes**

GRASSHOPPERS & CRICKETS
World Species: 19,000
NA Species: 1,080

No — **Is its head hidden by a part of the thorax, and does the head point downwards?** — **Yes**

COCKROACHES
World Species: 4,000
NA Species: 50

No

BEETLES
World Species: 370,000
NA Species: 24,000

Note

Before deciding whether an insect is winged or not, check out ants and termites. Only the reproductive males and females (the ones that can lay and fertilize eggs) have wings—the workers don't have them. Other insects also have wingless forms—you may have found a nymph (a still-developing insect.)

The blue box shows that these insects are usually found in or near water. This can be when they are immature, adult or both.

Found Almost Everywhere

The families that you will find in the following pages are either very common or truly widespread. Many of them you will easily find in parks and backyards, but many you may see everywhere from a city street to a seaside beach—and anywhere in between!

Backyards and parks are a very important habitat (type of landscape) for wildlife, especially now that gardeners are planting such a wide variety of plants. Different plants lead to lots of different insects, many of whom often eat from only one type of plant. Large numbers of insects encourage more insectivores, like birds and shrews, to live in the area.

A well-stocked, average-sized, urban yard (measuring about 2,000 square feet) may hold 200–300 different beetle species, up to 200 species of flies, of which more than fifty to sixty may be flies, and hundreds of bee and wasp species, including sixty or more species of solitary bees and wasps. In addition there may be eighty to ninety bug species, and more than 300 species of butterflies and moths (mostly moths.)

Remember as well that many of those insects may be simply passing through as tourists. This picture shows thirteen species from this section; see how many can you identify.

Ant, Leaf-cutter Bee, Assassin Bug, Shield Bug,
Painted Lady Butterfly, Humpbacked Fly, Hawk Moth,
Hover fly, Lacewing, Snout Moth, Tiger Moth,
Common Wasp, Weevil.

Found Almost Everywhere

Cockroaches

Many of these large, fast-running cockroaches are brown or reddish-brown with a shiny appearance. Their oval, flattened bodies let them hide in narrow crevices. Their legs are spiny. When running about, they continually wave their antennae. They are found both in the wild and in buildings in many habitats. A female *Periplaneta americana* (American Cockroach, shown here) may lay up to fifty egg cases—they look like tiny purses—containing 12–14 eggs. Some species emit a foul-smelling liquid.

Order: Blattodea
Family: Blattidae
NA species: 6
World species: 600
Body length: 1–1 3/4 ins

Jumping Bristletails

If you search under stones in grassy areas or woods, in rock or leaf litter, or on rocks on the seashore above the high-tide line, you should find some of these little bristletails. You may find *Petrobius maritimus* (shown here) running over rocks and harbor walls close to the sea. They look rather like silverfish (see page 74,) but are brownish in color with a humped thorax. If you disturb them, they jump before making for cover. They feed mainly on algae, mosses, lichens, and decaying organic debris.

Order: Archaeognatha
Family: Machilidae
NA species: 14
World species: 250
Body length: Up to 1/2 ins

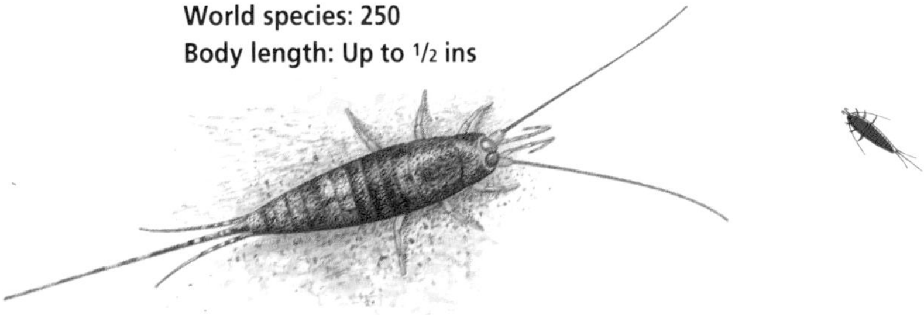

Common Earwigs

Species in this family are found in ground litter, soil, under loose bark, or in rocky crevices. If you search in such places, you will soon find them—often dozens of individuals clustered together. In some species the female stands guard over her eggs. This is an example of primitive maternal care. She even licks the eggs to keep them free of infection. The forceps at the tail-end are used for courtship and defense. Despite their name, they are very unlikely to get into human ears. Some species are garden pests because they chew flower petals. The commonest species, *Forficula auricularia* (European Earwig, shown here,) was introduced to the U.S. from Europe in the early 1900s.

Order: Dermaptera
Family: Forficulidae
NA species: 4
World species: 465
Body length: Up to 1 1/2 ins

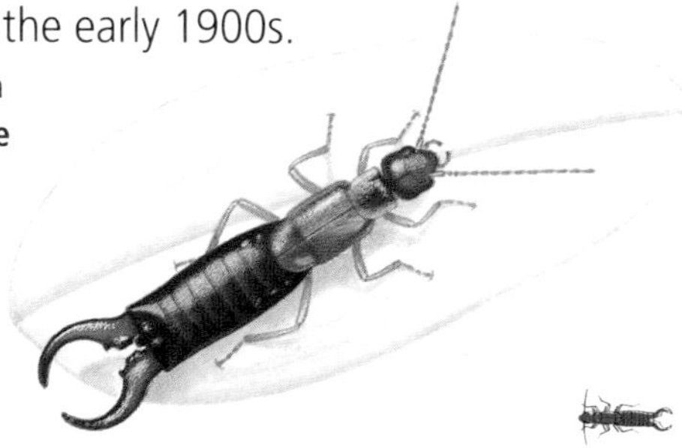

Tube-tailed Thrips

Members of this family are found in small habitats such as herbaceous plants, shrubs, trees, flowers, twigs, and under bark. Some dwell in leaf litter and soil. Although this family contains some of the world's largest thrips, most are less than 1/8 ins long. While the majority feed on fungal threads and the spores of fungi, some are carnivorous.

Order: Thysanoptera
Family: Phlaeothripidae
NA species: 348
World species: 2,700
Body length: 1/16–1/8 ins

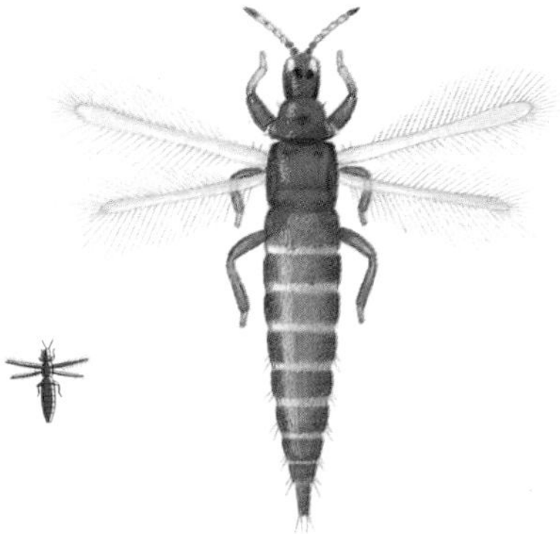

Haplothrips kurdjumovi

Ants

You can find ants in every color from pale yellow to black. They live in colonies and are adapted for their *Lasius niger* particular tasks. You will mostly see the wingless workers, but the queens, who lay the eggs, and the males, who fertilize them, have wings. Look for ants disappearing into holes in the ground in your backyard. They also live in natural cavities and build nests above ground. Search in conifer woods for the great mounds of leaves and pine needles that are the home of Wood Ants. Ants can be herbivores or carnivores, or mixed feeders (omnivores.) Many are addicted to the honeydew produced by aphids (see page 16) or the sap of plants. Some ants have powerful biting jaws. Others can sting you or spray formic acid, which stings.

**Order: Hymenoptera – Family: Formicidae – NA species: 600
World species: 8,800 – Body length: 1/16–3/4 ins**

Common Thrips

Like the previous family, common thrips are tiny. If you look carefully among flowerheads, peas, beans, and in the ears of cereals, you should find plenty of specimens. Despite their small size, they are important pests because they transmit virus diseases to many commercial crops. Sometimes these small insects are called thunderflies because they seem to fly around just before thunderstorms.

**Order: Thysanoptera
Family: Thripidae
NA species: 265
World species: 1,500
Body length: 1/16–1/8 ins**

***Limothrips cerealium* (Grain Thrip) is a
pest that breeds in the ears of cereal
crops. It is less than 1/8 ins long.**

Green or Common Lacewings

Green Lacewings are very common and you should easily be able to find some. They sometimes come to lighted windows and are mainly nocturnal. You will find them in all types of vegetation, where their prey—aphids, scale insects, and mites—live. Some species have incredible bat-detecting, ultrasonic sound receivers in the veins of their wings—a useful way to avoid being snatched out of the sky by a hungry bat. Green lacewings often hibernate in houses and attics.

**Order: Neuroptera
Family: Chrysopidae
NA species: 88
World species: 1,600
Body length: 1/4–1 ins**

***Chrysopa carnea* has bright golden, brassy or reddish eyes,
which seem to shine.**

True Crickets

These are found in all kinds of herbage in woodlands, scrub, meadows, and grassland. Most species hide away under stones, logs, or leaf litter. Others live in trees, while some live underground, but certain members of this family live in domestic situations. Some are active by day, others nocturnal. The species shown is *Acheta domesticus* (the House Cricket,) which was once very common in old houses and bakeries. It has been introduced to North America from Europe. Today, due to increased cleanliness and modern building methods, they are not found so often.

**Order: Orthoptera
Family: Gryllidae
NA species: 96
World species: 1,800
Body length: 1/8–13/4 ins**

Found Almost Everywhere

Carrion or Burying Beetles

Order: Coleoptera
Family: Silphidae
NA species: 42
World species: 250
Body length:
1/4–1 1/2 ins

These beetles have a very sensitive sense of smell and are attracted to the dead bodies of animals. The well-named *Nicrophorus vespilloides* (Sexton Beetle, shown here) is a good example of the family. The adult beetles are very strong and two can move an animal as big as a rat to a good location for burying. Their purpose in doing this is to lay eggs on or near the carcass so that the larvae have a plentiful food supply. They are very important in nutrient recycling and carcass disposal—some of the most efficient refuse collectors of the insect world.

Ground Beetles

These beetles have well-developed legs and powerful jaws. They live in a wide range of habitats under stones, wood, and debris. If you lift such objects, you may see one running away very fast. They catch and eat a large variety of invertebrates and carrion, although a few species feed on plants. Their larvae are also active hunters and live in soil and leaf litter. They have powerful jaws and use enzymes to dissolve their prey's insides. The adults of some species climb into trees and shrubs to catch and eat caterpillars.

Order: Coleoptera
Family: Carabidae
NA species: 2,270
World species: 25,000
Body length: 1/16–3 1/4 ins

Calosoma sycophanta

Rove Beetles

This family has very many species. Most are quite small and can run fast. Small species fly by day, while larger ones fly at night. This is a family of predators, scavengers, or herbivores. By searching under stones you may find a *Staphylinus olens* (Devil's Coach-horse, shown here.) 300 species of rove beetles are associated with ants. They mimic their hosts and will offer them a sweet fluid to avoid attack. But they prey on hurt or dead ants.

Order: Coleoptera – Family: Staphylinidae
NA species: 3,200 – World species: 27,000
Body length: 1/16–1 1/2 ins

Sap Beetles

Look at daisies and their flowers for these beetles. The adults feed on sap oozing from tree wounds, on flower nectar, decaying fruits, carrion, and other rotting matter. Some species are associated with ants and bees. Anybody who wears yellow clothes in the summer may find they attract members of this family. They can ruin picnics and also seem to be attracted to bright, fresh paint. A few species prey on scale insects, and some feed inside plant seed-pods.

Order: Coleoptera
Family: Nitidulidae
NA species: 185
World species: 2,800
Body length: 1/16–1/2 ins

Meligethes aeneus
(Pollen Beetle)

Leaf Beetles

Members of this family are to be found on every plant species and in all land habitats. The adults chew flowers and foliage. Their larvae feed in the same way, but also mine and bore through leaves, stems, and roots. Many of these smooth, rounded, and often shiny or colorful beetles are serious pests. This is the notorious *Leptinotarsa decemlineata* (Colorado Potato Beetle.) This species attacks potatoes, tomatoes, and eggplants. Some leaf beetle species can be useful in controlling weeds.

Order: Coleoptera
Family: Chrysomelidae
NA species: 1,480
World species: 30,000
Body length: 1/16–11/2 ins

Snout Beetles or Weevils

The species of this gigantic family are by far the commonest insects on Earth. All weevils have a snout or "rostrum" which carries the jaws. The family has members associated with almost every species of plant. Nearly all are herbivorous and they eat every bit of a plant, from root to seed. If disturbed, they usually lie quite still, or else fold their legs beneath their body and simply fall to the ground, as if they were dead. Many species, like the Grain Weevil (*Sitophillus granarius*, shown here,) are serious pests. The Cotton Boll Weevil is the major pest species attacking the American cotton crop.

Order: Coleoptera
Family: Curculionidae
NA species: 2,700
World species: 41,000
Body length: 1/16–2 ins

Checkered Beetles

Most of this family have soft, slightly flattened bodies which are very hairy. Their coloring can be bright blue, green, red, brown or pink. Checkered beetles are to be found on the leaves of woody plants and in woody areas. The larvae prey on the larvae of bark beetles and other bark-boring beetles. Some others prey on the larvae of bees and wasps, and on grasshopper egg-pods. Some species are able to find their prey by the pheromes (scents) they produce. *Necrobia rufipes* (the Redlegged Ham Beetle, shown here) can damage stored meat and meat products.

Order: Coleoptera
Family: Cleridae
NA species: 270
World species: 3,500
Body length: 1/16–11/8 ins

Found Almost Everywhere

Dance Flies

The common name of this predacious family comes from the mating swarms that occur in summer in which males fly up and down in a dancing fashion. They feed by catching small flies. Males sometimes offer prey items to females to eat while they mate with them. Some dance flies take prey from spiders' webs. Their habitat is moist places near water. Their larvae live in humus, leaf litter, decaying wood and vegetation, under bark, and in water. They eat black fly, scale insects, and mites. Much remains to be discovered about these insects.

Order: Diptera – Family: Empidae – NA species: 730
World species: 3,500 – Body length: 1/16–1/2 ins

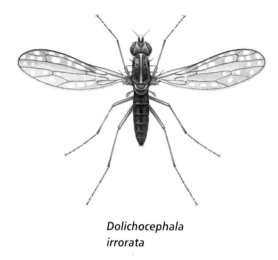

Dolichocephala irrorata

Blow Flies

Typical species of this family are the familiar bluebottle and greenbottle flies. They have metallic green or blue, shiny black or dull coloration. In some species, the sexes are of different colors. You have most probably seen one when it flew indoors attracted to your food. Adults feed on flower pollen and nectar, as well as rotting animal and plant matter. Being fond of carrion (rotting meat) and dung makes them carriers of diseases such as dysentery. A very unpleasant species lays its eggs on the wool of sheep. The larvae then bore into the flesh of the sheep, leaving terrible wounds. Other species attack worms, and still others suck the blood of nestling birds.

Order: Diptera
Family: Calliphoridae
NA species: 80
World species: 1,200
Body length: 1/8–1/2 ins

Calliphora vomitoria

Syrphid Flies

On any sunny day during the summer you will be able to see syrphid flies. Spend a while watching their amazing aerial acrobatics. They can move suddenly in any direction, including backward, or hover over a flower head. Look for them on flat-topped flower clusters as they feed on pollen and nectar. Although they look like bees and wasps, they cannot hurt you because they do not sting. In North America the larvae of *Mesogramma polita* sometimes damage corn crops, but the larvae of most species are useful and eat thousands of insects, especially aphids.

Order: Diptera
Family: Syrphidae
NA species: 870
World species: 6,000
Body length: 1/8–1 1/2 ins

Syrphus vitripennis can hover like a tiny helicopter.

Humpbacked Flies

With their humped backs these small flies scuttle about on compost heaps, rotting fungi, and around the nests of rodents and ants. If you use your sweep net in such locations, you may find one scuttling among the assorted flies you have caught. They are quite small, but you should be able to find some where you live. As with all small insects, you need to observe closely and patiently. The larvae of some of these flies are internal parasites of other insects, spiders, snails, or millipedes. A few are pests of cultivated mushrooms.

Order: Diptera
Family: Phoridae
NA species: 360
World species: 2,800
Body length: 1/16–1/4 ins

Megaselia pleuralis

Moth & Sand Flies

Both families are widely distributed through many habitats. The larval form of many species is unknown, and many other psychodid species remain undescribed. Some moth flies, which are sometimes called owl midges (subfamily: Psychodinae,) are nocturnal and are attracted to lights. You may find some on your windows in spring and summer. Adult moth flies do not bite.

Sand flies (subfamily: Phlebotominae) feed on the blood of humans and many other vertebrates. They also carry unpleasant diseases in many tropical and subtropical regions of the world.

Order: Diptera
Family: Psychodidae
NA species: 91
World species: 1,000
Body length: 1/16–1/4 ins

 Psychoda alternata

Leaf-mining Flies

You are more likely to find the signs of their larvae than to see the adults, simply because these flies have no easy recognition features. The adults lay their eggs in plant tissue and the larvae make mines between the upper and lower leaf surfaces. Species of *Liriomyza* are very destructive to tomatoes, cucumbers, squashes, celery, and other important plant species in North America. If you search through the leaves of holly between September and May, you should be able to find the work of the Holly Leaf Miner. Try keeping some mined leaves from a variety of plants in a sealed container (see page 65.) In a while the adult flies, and even some of their parasites, will appear.

Agromyza reptans

Order: Diptera – Family: Agromyzidae – NA species: 493
World species: 2,500 – Body length: 1/16–1/4 ins

Muscid Flies

You have certainly seen one of these flies land on the window or your food, or noticed them walking upside-down on the ceiling. As they feed on decaying material and excrement, many of them spread diseases like cholera, typhoid fever, and dysentery. The female lays eggs in masses on rotting plant or animal matter. In about a week they hatch into larvae, which are commonly known as maggots. While we may not like the habits of the *Musca domestica* (House Fly, shown here,) we should try to appreciate how perfectly they are adapted to their way of life.

Order: Diptera
Family: Muscidae
NA species: 622
World species: 3,000
Body length: 1/16–1/2 ins

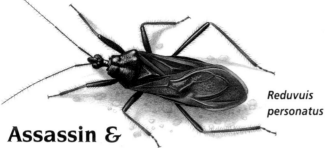

Reduvuis personatus

Assassin & Thread-legged Bugs

Vegetation of all kinds provides habitat for this family. They are well named because they hunt and kill all kinds of insects by sucking out their juices. A few species suck the blood of birds and mammals. Some species lie in wait to ambush prey, while others actively hunt for their food. Many species mimic the appearance and color pattern of their prey. A few assassin bug species collect plant resins on their front legs to attract and snare prey.

Order: Hemiptera – Family: Reduviidae – NA species: 110
World species: 5,500 – Body length: 1/4–1 1/2 ins

Leafhoppers

A massive family—it is thought that almost every plant species has at least one species of leafhopper eating it. All of them suck plant juices. The (Redbanded Leafhopper (*Graphocephala fennahi*, shown here) is found on blackberry and other ornamental plants in North America. Females lay up to 300 eggs in the tissues of the host plant. The nymphs produce large amounts of honeydew, which certain species, known as sharpshooters, can expel rapidly or spot on to leaves. Many species produce up to five distinct types of sound. In this way they recognize their own species and find a mate. Many species are serious pests of crops and other important plants.

Order: Hemiptera – Family: Cicadellidae
NA species: 2,700
World species: 21,000
Body length: 1/8–3/4 ins

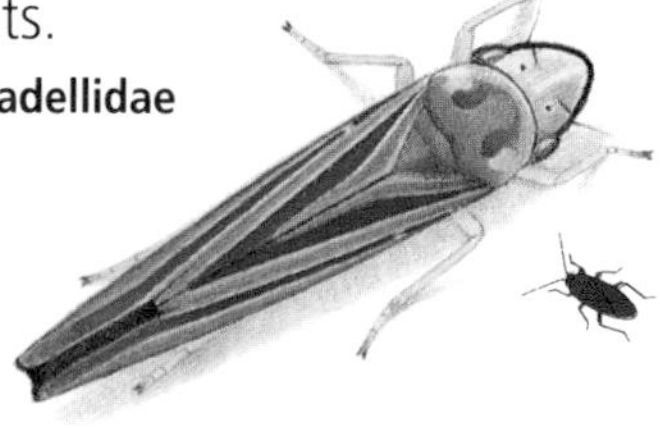

Plant Lice or Aphids

You can nearly always see these tiny insects on plants—they are found almost anywhere. They are all suckers of plant sap. Aphids are pests on just about every crop and cultivated plant species. They also damage plants by passing on virus diseases. Because they suck in so much sweet plant sap, they produce lots of sugary waste. This "honeydew" is often collected by ants.

Order: Hemiptera
Family: Aphididae
NA species: 1,350
World species: 2,250
Body length: 1/16–1/4 ins

Aphis fabae
(Garden Black Fly)

Treehoppers

Many treehoppers have strange humps, spines and other projections from the back of the thorax. If you touch one gently, you will see it hop. Some species look very much like thorns, as does the *Stictocephala bisonia* (American Buffalo Treehopper, shown here,) and this disguise helps them to pass unnoticed as part of a plant. This species was introduced to Europe early this century, and is often found on apples, willow, hawthorn, and lime. The nymphs of all species excrete honeydew, and many are attended by ants who gather the sweet liquid. In return, the ants guard the treehopper nymphs from attack. There is evidence of maternal care, the females of many species guarding the young nymphs from attack.

Order: Hemiptera
Family: Membracidae
NA species: 258
World species: 2,500
Body length: 1/4–1/2 ins

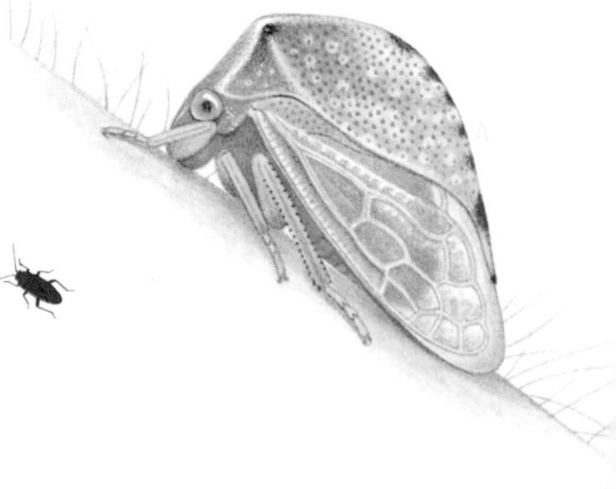

Psyllids

Each species belonging to this family lives on one, or a few, closely related plants. Some lay stalked eggs on plant surfaces, while others lay eggs inside plants. All members of this family are important pests because they are sap-suckers. They can also transmit virus diseases to plants such as tomatoes, potatoes, apples, and pears. *Psylla pyricola* (the Pear Sucker, shown here) is a pest on pear crops. Some members of this family also cause galls to form on leaves. These insects use their hind legs to jump.

Order: Hemiptera – Family: Psyllidae – NA species: 260
World species: 1,500 – Body length: 1/16–1/4 ins

Minute Pirate Bugs

This is a family that lives in a variety of habitats, such as in flowers, under bark, in vegetation, leaf litter, and fungi. Others live in mammals' burrows, bird nests, bat caves, and grain stores. Many prey on small insects, while others are herbivorous (they eat plants.) Despite their very small size they can give a very nasty bite if handled roughly. Some species are useful because they eat red spider mites, aphids, and scale insects (see page 75.)

Order: Hemiptera
Family: Anthocoridae
NA species: 85
World species: 500
Body length: 1/16–1/4 ins

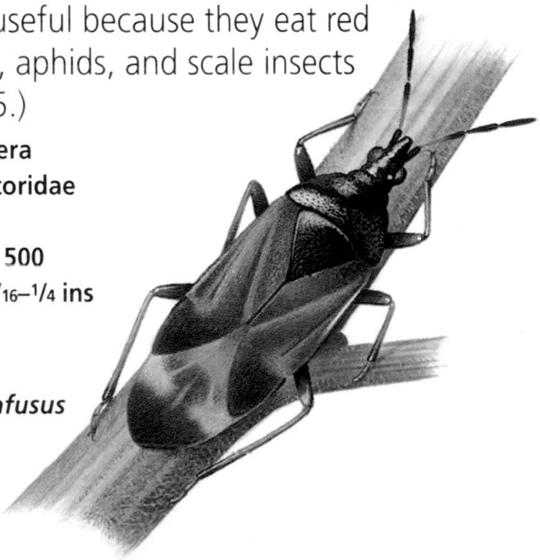

Anthocoris confusus

Plant Bugs

A family found in every habitat from ground level to tree tops and on every type of vegetation. This family is the largest of the true bugs. The habits of various species vary enormously. You may come across some by simply looking carefully on plants, or perhaps find some in your beating tray (see page 53.) A few species give off scents, which are like the alarm scents given off by ants—a good protective device. Some species can feed on prey caught in spider webs.

Order: Hemiptera
Family: Miridae
NA species: 1,950
World species: 7,000
Body length: 1/16–1/2 ins

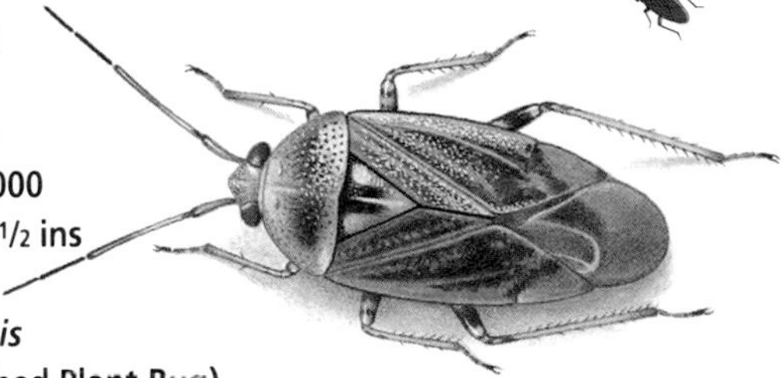

Lygus rugulipennis
(European Tarnished Plant Bug)

Stink Bugs

The common name for these insects comes from their ability to produce very strong-smelling fluids. These fluids repel enemies, can stain skin, and even produce bad headaches in sensitive people. Stink bugs live on herbaceous plants, shrubs, and trees in a wide range of habitats. Most are herbivores (plant-eaters,) but some are carnivorous. In many species the female will guard her eggs and shepherd the young nymphs together, covering them with her body when danger threatens.

Order: Hemiptera
Family: Pentatomidae
NA species: 250
World species: 5,250
Body length: 1/4–1 1/2 ins

Zicrona caerulea
(Blue Bug)

Common, Paper, & Potter Wasps

These are easy to recognize as "real" wasps, or yellow jackets, in their black with yellow or white markings. They are some of nature's most elegant architects. Their nests, where a queen, males, and sterile female workers form a social colony, are made by the workers chewing up wood fibers or paper. They feed their larvae on chewed insects, which they capture alive. The adults feed on nectar and other sugar-rich foods.

Potter wasps do not live in colonies. They collect mud or clay and make vase-shaped nests under ground, or in plant stems. They then paralyze a caterpillar and suspend it from the roof as preserved food for the larva. Watch them but be careful not to touch: they sting.

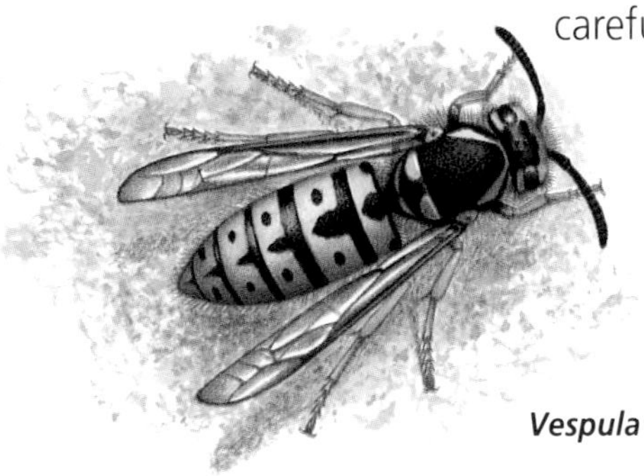

Order: Hymenoptera
Family: Vespidae
NA species: 415
World- species: 3,800
Body length: 1/4–1 ins

Vespula germanica

Leaf-cutter & Mason Bees

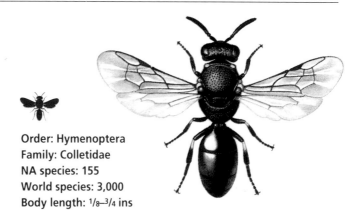

Members of this large family of bees are common everywhere in areas where there is plenty of dead wood or pithy plant stems to provide nest sites. Most species are solitary. They collect mud, resin, leaf matter, or plant hairs to line their larval cells. If you search carefully on rose bushes in parks or yards during June and July, you may find almost circular holes cut into the leaves. This is the work of a leaf-cutter bee.

Megachile rotundata (the Alfalfa Leaf-cutter Bee, shown above) was accidentally introduced from Eastern Europe to North America. It is now managed commercially for alfalfa pollination.

Mason bees dig their cells into mud beneath stones, on earth banks, and occasionally in galls. Some species of this family are important pollinators of crops and other plants.

Order: Hymenoptera – Family: Megachilidae – NA species: 682
World species: 3,000 – Body length: 1/4–3/4 ins

Plasterer & Yellow-faced Bees

If you use your hand lens, you may see the branched or feathered body hairs which are characteristic of these and all other families of bees.

Plasterer bees make simple nest burrows in the ground, or in natural cavities in stones and bricks.

Yellow-faced bees nest in the pith of plant stems, the empty burrows of wood-boring insects, and plant galls. Unlike plasterer bees, they do not have pollen baskets on their legs; instead they swallow the pollen with nectar to carry it to their nest. They then bring it up to fill the larval cells with food.

Order: Hymenoptera
Family: Colletidae
NA species: 155
World species: 3,000
Body length: 1/8–3/4 ins

Hylaeus bisinuatus is a yellow-faced bee, although it doesn't have a yellow face.

Mining or Andrenid Bees

Look for these bees in any flower-filled habitat in spring and early summer. As early as March you will see them on dandelions, daisies, and willow catkins. You may find tiny mounds of soil—signs of their burrow-building—on your lawn or in grassy, sunny banks. Although they are solitary bees, some species tend to make their burrows in large groups. They put pellets of mixed pollen and honey in their burrows as food for the larvae. Some species are parasitized by the well-named cuckoo bees (see page 50.) These bees are common pollinators of spring flowers.

Order: Hymenoptera
Family: Andrenidae
NA species: 1,200
World species: 4,000
Body length: 1/8–3/4 ins

Andrena clarkella

Halictid or Sweat Bees

Only some species are attracted to sweat in addition to the normal diet of pollen and nectar. The bees in this family will sting, but it is not very painful. Some species are solitary; others are semi-social. The female is long-lived and often guards her pollen-stored cells until the young bees emerge. Most make burrows in firm soil, such as garden paths, especially with clay or sandy soils. The species *Halictus ribicundus* (shown here) is a typical member of this family.

Order: Hymenoptera
Family: Halictidae
NA species: 502
World species: 5,000
Body length: 1/8–1/2 ins

Bumblebees & Honey Bees

Bumblebees are those large, furry, buzzing bees that visit flowers throughout the summer. In sunny weather in March and April, watch for a large queen bumble that has just come out of winter hibernation. She will make a mossy nest on or under the ground. Her 300 or 400 eggs will first produce sterile worker bees to build up the colony and collect food.

Bombus lucorum

Honey bees are much smaller and often start a colony in a hollow tree or roof space. They are also kept in hives by bee-keepers. A single queen may lay tens of thousands of eggs to produce workers, and up to 2,000 males or drones. Honey bees collect nectar and pollen from flowers. They store pollen and the honey they make from nectar in thousands of wax cells which make a comb.

Order: Hymenoptera – Family: Apidae – NA species: 57
World species: 1,000 – Body length: 1/8–1 ins

Common Sawflies

Sawflies are, of course, not flies at all. They are in the same insect order as wasps, ants, and bees. Unlike those creatures, sawflies have no waist. Their name refers to the saw-like ovipositor (egg-laying organ) of the females. With it they cut slits in leaves, twigs or shoots of their host plants and lay their eggs there.

Order: Hymenoptera
Family: Tenthredinidae
NA species: 735
World species: 4,000
Body length: 1/8–3/4 ins

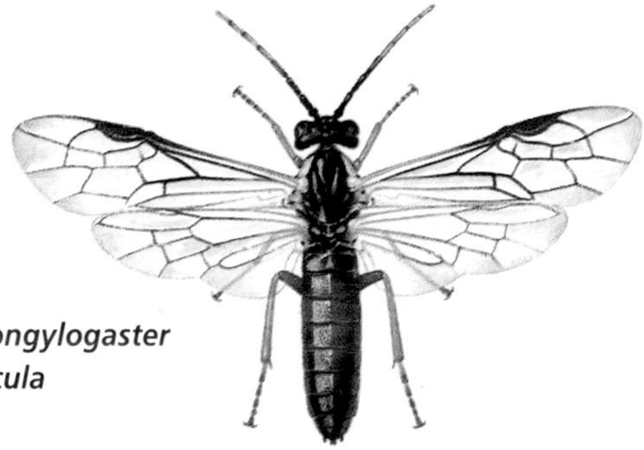

Strongylogaster macula

Gossamer-winged Butterflies

We do not know a lot about the life cycles of many of these brilliantly colored, iridescent blue, copper or purplish butterflies. About one-third live in association with ants in a variety of habitats. The butterfly larvae produce a sugary fluid which the ants eat. In return the ants guard them. The caterpillars of some species even feed on the larvae in the ants' nest. As many of this family are very beautiful, they have been overcollected and are close to extinction. Many are now protected by law.

Order: Lepidoptera
Family: Lycaenidae
NA species: 138
World species: 6,000
Wingspan: ½–2 ins

Lycaena phlaeas
(American Copper)

Tiger & Ermine Moths

Tiger moths are mainly nocturnal, heavy-bodied, hairy, and often brightly colored. The bright colors are a warning to their predators that they are distasteful; some are even poisonous. The best time to search for *Arctia caja* (the Garden Tiger Moth, shown here) is when it is on the wing in July and August. *Tyria jacobaea* (the Cinnabar Moth) has been introduced from Europe to North American Pacific states to control Klamath weed.

Ermine moths tend to be pale or white with small black spots or patches. Due to the variety of their food plants, they are to be found in a wide variety of habitats. The caterpillars are covered with hairs that cause a rash in humans.

Order: Lepidoptera
Family: Arctiidae
NA species: 264
World species: 2,500
Wingspan: ¾–2¾ ins

Agonopterix heracliana

Oecophorid Moths

Most of these moths can be found in a variety of habitats in association with their host plants. A very few species are to be found indoors where they may be pests of woollens and other textiles. Not much is known about the caterpillars of some species, but some eat plants or are fungus feeders, and others may feed on decaying matter.

Order: Lepidoptera
Family: Oecophoridae
NA species: 230
World species: 3,500
Wingspan: 1/4–1 1/8 ins

Brush Footed Butterflies

A family of beautiful and colorful butterflies, most of which are common. Every sunny day you can see them flying and visiting flowers to drink the nectar. They are found everywhere—especially in flower-rich meadows, woodland clearings, and yards. Their caterpillars are generally spiny and feed on nettles, thistles, sunflowers and other plants. Look among stinging nettles in July and August and you should find larvae of the Red Admiral and Mourning Cloak butterflies. Members of this family, like *Cynthia cardui* (the Painted Lady, shown here,) undertake migrations, and some species, like the Small Tortoiseshell, hibernate.

Order: Lepidoptera
Family: Nymphalidae
NA species: 140
World species: 3,500
Wingspan: 1 1/8–4 1/4 ins

Tortricid Moths

Species of this large family of smallish moths show a multitude of cryptic patterns on their wings. Some of the patterns make them look like bark, others resemble lichen, bird droppings, and bits of leaves. They are found in a wide variety of habitats. There are many pest species in the family, notably the Codling Moth (*Cydia pomonella,* shown here,) introduced to North America over 200 years ago. The caterpillars of some species bore into stems and leaves, and a few cause galls.

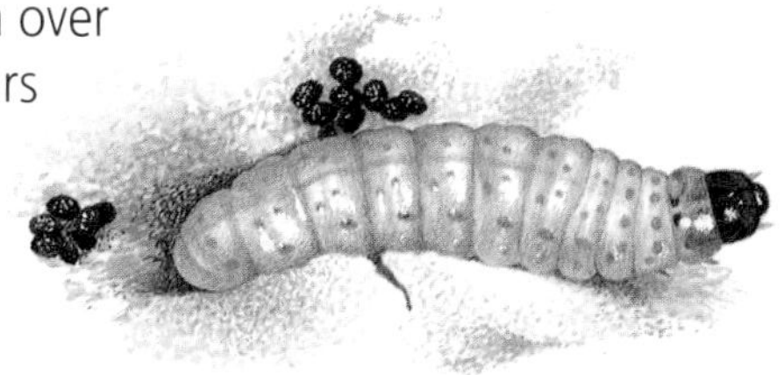

Order: Lepidoptera
Family: Tortricidae
NA species: 1,060
World species: 4,500
Wingspan: 1/4–1 1/4 ins

Pyralid Moths

The front wings of this family are usually oblong or triangular with closely packed scales. In some species the front of the head looks as if it has a small snout. This is the third largest family of moths, so there is a huge range of color, shape, and size in the different species. Many are pests: the caterpillar of *Ostrina nubilalis* (the European Corn-borer, adult shown here) damages young corn. This species was accidentally introduced to North America early this century. Others attack corn, sunflowers, apples, cabbage, and other food crops.

Order: Lepidoptera
Family: Pyralidae
NA species: 1,380
World species: 17,500
Wingspan: 1/2–1 1/2 ins

White, Sulfur, & Orange Tip Butterflies

This family contains some of the world's most common butterflies. Their habitats range from woodlands to meadows and from mountains to sea level. Caterpillars of the best-known species feed on the cabbage family. In good summer weather Small Whites breed so fast that they become pests on cabbage crops. This species is one of the most crop-damaging butterflies. It was introduced to North America from Europe over 100 years ago. Other species feed on alder, hawthorn, and willows. Look for Orange Tips flying along hedges in early summer. Search for the Sulfurs (also known as Brimstones) along hedges with some buckthorn bushes.

Order: Lepidoptera
Family: Pieridae
NA species: 65
World species: 1,300
Wingspan: 3/4–2 3/4 ins

Pieris rapae
(Small White)

Noctuid Moths

Species from this enormous family of moths can be found all over the world. With a medium-sized wingspan, mostly 1³/₄–2¹/₂ ins, they are dull in color with narrowish front wings. The antennae are hair-like in females, but brush-like in males. Males often have a tuft of hairs at the end of the abdomen. They fly at night and are to be found in almost every kind of habitat. They have thoracic hearing organs which help the moths to detect and avoid bats. *Agrotis ipsilon* (the Dark Sword-grass Moth, shown here) is widespread in North America.

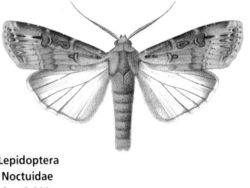

Order: Lepidoptera
Family: Noctuidae
NA species: 3,000
World species: 25,000
Wingspan: ¹/₂–3¹/₈ ins

Geometer Moths

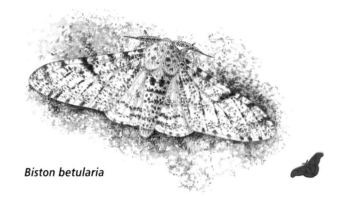

Biston betularia

The caterpillars of this enormous family move by a looping motion. They draw their hind end up to meet the front end in a loop, then push the front end forward. This gives them their family name, Geometridae, meaning earth-measuring. The adult moths can be found almost everywhere that plants grow, and in summer many will fly in and settle on lighted windows. Very many species are pests of trees and crops. The Winter Moth, *Operophtera brumata* (shown here,) is a typical pest species, introduced to North America from Europe. It particularly damages apple trees.

Order: Lepidoptera – Family: Geometridae – NA species: 1,400
World species: 18,000 – Wingspan: ¹/₂–1³/₄ ins

Sphinx or Hawk Moths

The moths in this family rest with swept-back wings, like the wings of a fighter plane. Many species visit garden and park flowers, such as petunias, at dusk. Hawk moths' habitats cover a great variety of wooded and open areas, including backyards and parks, where their food—plants, trees, and flowers—may grow. Some species are serious crop pests. The *Manduca quinquemaculata* (Tomato Hornworm) of North America and the *Manduca sexta* (Tobacco Hornworm) are examples. Most species in this family are nocturnal feeders.

Order: Lepidoptera
Family: Sphingidae
NA species: 124
World species: 1,200
Wingspan: 1¹/₂–6 ins

Hyles lineata (Striped Hawk Moth)

An Insect Safari

There are insects everywhere on Earth, from the frozen tundra plains to the jungles and deserts of the tropics. There are more than 1.5 million species of animals in the world, ranging from the primitive amoebas to humans. Of these species, over 932,000—or nearly two-thirds of all the known species—are insects. On every square mile of land, there will be thousands of millions of insects to be found.

Insect watching

A good time to study insects such as bees, wasps, dragonflies, and butterflies is on a warm, sunny day when there is no wind. If you want to watch nighttime (nocturnal) insects such as moths, a warm, still summer evening is best.

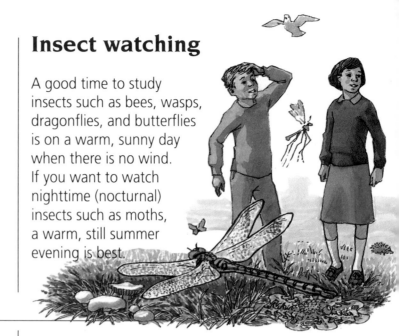

What to take

When you go looking for insects, it is a good idea to take these pieces of equipment with you:

1. **Magnifying lens**: helps you to look at small insects close up and in great detail. Buy a folding one that magnifies things 4 or 6 times (labeled x4 or x6.) Wear it on a cord around your neck.
2. **Glass or plastic jars with holes bored in the lid:** useful if you find a large insect and want to put it somewhere safe while you look at it.
3. **Pooter:** see opposite for how to make one.
4. **Aerial net:** for trapping butterflies and moths temporarily.
5. **Beating tray or a pale umbrella:** for investigating trees and bushes (see page 53.)
6. **Field notebook with pencils and pens:** make notes of the date, the weather, where you go, and what you find.
7. **Lightweight backpack:** this is the most comfortable way to carry your equipment, and leaves your hands free.

Making a pooter

A pooter helps you to pick up and look at bugs and other small insects without harming them. It is quite easy to make a pooter of your own.

1 **Take a piece of clear plastic** 4 inches square and roll it into a tube. Secure it with some Scotch tape.

2 **You will also need two wide drinking straws** and a piece of gauze 2½ inches square. Place the gauze over the end of one of the straws and tape it in position.

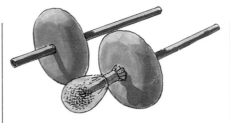

3 **Find some modeling clay or Plasticine** and make two round blobs, each about the size of a ping-pong ball. Squash them flat into disc shapes, then push one straw through the middle of each.

4 **Put one disk at each end of the plastic tube**, so that the gauze is inside the tube.

5 **When you suck at the straw with gauze on the other end,** air will rush into the plastic pooter through the other straw. If you then gently hold your pooter close to a bug and suck on the straw, the insect will be caught safely and quickly.

6 **Once you have finished looking,** release the insect by removing one end of the pooter. Always try to put insects back where you found them.

7 **Remember to use your pooter carefully,** and never try to catch spiders or large insects like butterflies, as you could harm them.

Where to look

You probably don't need to look far on your insect safari to see a beetle on the ground or a bee at a flower. You can find other kinds of insects on leaves, plant stems, under stones, and under loose tree bark. Spend some time watching the insects that you find to see where they go and what they do. If you look carefully, you will learn lots more about the way they live.

Look under leaves to find insects like shield bugs.

Look under paving stones in your yard to find ants' nests.

Look on plant stems to find insects like aphids and ladybugs.

Look under loose tree bark to find insects like earwigs.

Look under rotting logs to find insects like beetles.

Grasslands

Wide, open grasslands once stretched from the Appalachians to the Rockies, covering much of North America. Most of this land is now planted with crops, and only remnants of the original grasslands remain.

But you will also find prairies in the Southwest, California, and between the Rockies, the Sierra Nevada, and the Cascade range. There are two kinds of grassland in the prairies: short grass in the West, changing to tall grass in the East. Tall grass is spectacular, particularly in spring when the wild flowers are out. This habitat includes hedges and roadsides—all grassy areas rich in wild flowers. This picture shows nine species from this section; see how many you can identify.

Soldier Beetle, Tumbling Flower Beetle, Milkweed Butterfly, Seed Bug, Ensign Fly, Short-horned Grasshopper, Plant Hopper, Mantis, Stem Sawfly.

Soldier Beetles

Order: Coleoptera
Family: Cantharidae
NA species: 468
World species: 4,000
Body length: 1/8–1 1/8 ins

Cantharis rustica

Some species of this family are very common, so you should quite easily find a few. In warm sunshine, look on flowers, along roadsides, and at the edge of woodland. The common family name comes from the resemblance of their coloring to old military uniforms. Although the adults of some species eat pollen and nectar, adults and their larvae hunt for prey on the ground. The soldier beetle in the picture can be found on grass and nettles, especially if you search for it in early summer. Birds rarely attack them—this is probably because of the beetle's bright yellow, red, or orange warning colors and nasty taste.

Tumbling Flower Beetles

Order: Coleoptera
Family: Mordellidae
NA species: 207
World species: 1,250
Body length: 1/16–2/3 ins

Look for these beetles on plants of the daisy family and on flowers with flat tops like cow-parsnip and wild carrot. In warm sun they may be found at rest on tree trunks. The reason for their common name is their habit of tumbling off their resting place when disturbed. Adults feed at flowers, but some of their larvae burrow in plant stems or live in decaying wood, while others bore inside fungi. Members of this family are not pests.

Tomoxia biguttata

Earth-boring Dung Beetles

As their name suggests, these beetles are found beneath dung of all kinds, on carrion, and in decaying wood or fungi. The adults dig out burrows many inches deep and stock these tunnels with balls of dung. A single egg is laid on each ball. The larva feeds on the dung. Some species feed on plant material, but most of the family are valuable as scavengers and dung removers. Look for them about sunset time on a warm evening.

Order: Coleoptera
Family: Geotrupidae
NA species: 51
World species: 550
Body length: 1/4–1 2/3 ins

Geotrupes stercorarius (the Common Dor Beetle.) The word "dor" comes from the ancient word meaning "drone," and refers to the humming flight of the beetle. It flies in the evening and is attracted to light.

Grasslands

Fruit Flies

Search for these quite beautiful flies around flowers and vegetation. You may be fortunate enough to watch their courtship behavior. The males of many species walk to and fro in front of the females. As they do so, they slowly wave one of their attractively patterned wings while holding the other upright. Many of their larvae live inside soft fruits, in the flower heads of daisies and related plants, or as stem- and leaf-miners and gall-formers. As pest species, some attack citrus fruits, peaches, cherries, apples, walnuts, and melons. *Ceratitis capitata* (the Mediterranean Fruit Fly, shown here) is a very serious pest in subtropical and tropical regions.

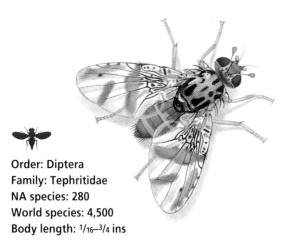

Order: Diptera
Family: Tephritidae
NA species: 280
World species: 4,500
Body length: 1/16–3/4 ins

Some species cause galls to form on thistles. You may find some if you search carefully. Each gall contains several growing larvae.

March Flies

Order: Diptera
Family: Bibionidae
NA species: 78
World species: 780
Body length:
1/4–1/2 ins

These insects were originally called St. Mark's flies because they are seen on the wing in swarms around April 25, which is the feast day of St. Mark. The females lay 200–300 eggs below ground, and their larvae eat all kinds of organic material and plant roots. Their habitats are backyards, flower-rich pastures and similar places. *Bibio marci* (shown here) is a typical member of the family. You may see one or more of these hairy-bodied flies flying slowly on a sunny April day with its legs dangling down.

Frit Flies

Their habitat is grassy meadows and among overgrown plants, flowers and decaying organic matter. The adults of this family eat nectar, prey on root aphids, or eat the eggs of spiders, moths, and other insects. A few, however, are important pests of farm crops. The larvae of most species are herbivorous. Those of *Oscinella frit* (shown here) damage cereal ears by boring into them.

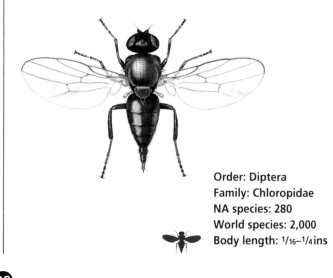

Order: Diptera
Family: Chloropidae
NA species: 280
World species: 2,000
Body length: 1/16–1/4 ins

Soldier Flies

A family of robust, metallic-sheened flies favoring a damp habitat. Look for them sitting on flowers of willow and hawthorn and flowers with flat tops, like water hemlock. You may hear some flying with a wasp-like hum over marshy ground from June to August. The name Soldier Fly comes from their armor of spines on various body parts. Some of their larvae, living under bark, may control bark beetles (see page 38.)

Order: Diptera
Family: Stratiomyidae
NA species: 260
World species: 1,800
Body length: 1/16–2/3 ins

Sargus cuprarius

Black Scavenger Flies

Members of this family are to be seen on flowers, vegetation and around dung or decaying plant and animal matter. Adult males display their wing tips by walking to and fro and flicking their wings outward. This is done to attract females. Whenever you are watching an insect, look out for interesting behavior. Make notes in your field notebook when you observe something (see page 24.)

Order: Diptera
Family: Sepsidae
NA species: 35
World species: 250
Body length: 1/16–1/4 ins

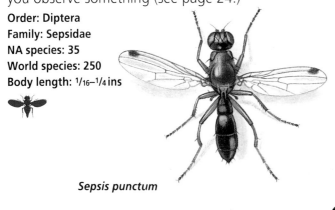

Sepsis punctum

Anthomyiid Flies

This is a very large family of rather ordinary-looking flies, which somewhat resemble house flies. Their adult food varies, ranging from pollen and nectar to small insects. Some of their larvae may be found as stem-borers, gall-formers and leaf-miners, while others live in rotting seaweed or bird droppings. A few species of *Delia* damage onions, turnips, cabbage, grain, and carnations, and have become serious pests. Since they are so common, it should not be too long before you see one.

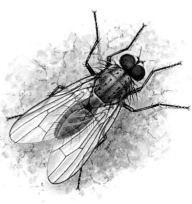

Delia platura

Order: Diptera – Family: Anthomyiidae – NA species: 600
World species: 1,500 – Body length: 1/16–1/2 ins

Dung Flies

You are most likely to encounter these flies around pasture land and farms where cattle are kept. They are best avoided because they carry disease germs on their feet. Not all the family lay eggs in dung. Some, in complete contrast, are laid in orchids and lilies. Adult dung flies all kill and eat small insects. It is perhaps a little odd that the family are called dung flies when many are not associated with dung. While the habits of many flies may seem unpleasant to us, their way of life helps to recycle materials back into the ecosystem.

Order: Diptera
Family: Scathophagidae
NA species: 148
World species: 250
Body length: 1/8–1/2 ins

Scathophaga stercoraria
(Yellow Dung Fly)

Grasslands

Spittle Bugs

In summer you have probably seen a small, white, frothy mass on grass stems and leaves. It is often called "cuckoo spit." If you take a grass stem and gently stroke away the bubbles, you will discover the nymph of a spittle bug. The foam, which acts as a sort of bubble-nest protection, is a glandular secretion mixed with the bug's waste (honeydew). Some birds have learned to pull the nymphs out and eat them. Adult spittle bugs, like froghoppers (see opposite,) are active jumpers. In North America two species attack pines.

Order: Hemiptera
Family: Aphrophoridae
NA species: 23
World species: 850
Body length: 1/4–1/2 ins

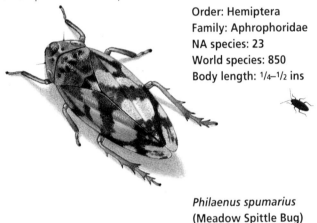

Philaenus spumarius
(Meadow Spittle Bug)

Delphacid Planthoppers

This family is common everywhere in grassland, meadows, pastures, and woodland margins. Adults and nymphs feed on plant sap. Although grasses and sedges (wetland grasses) are their main host plants, they also attack other plants. Some species have become serious crop pests; the Sugar-cane Leafhopper, for example, was accidentally introduced from Australia to Hawaii, where it caused terrible damage to sugar-canes. It was brought under control by using a small plant bug that sucked the eggs of the leafhopper. *Peregrinus maidis* (the Corn Hopper) spreads virus disease in corn throughout North America.

Order: Hemiptera
Family: Delphacidae
NA species: 145
World species: 1,800
Body length: 1/16–1/3 ins

Javesella pellucida

Scentless Plant Bugs

You may find members of this family on weeds and overgrown vegetation in old fields and other similar undisturbed habitats. These bugs lack scent glands, which is how the family gets its common name. A few live in trees, so look out for one when tree-beating. Like so many other bugs, they suck the juices of leaves, seeds, and fruit of their host plants. The best time to look for them is late summer and early fall. The *Liorhyssus hyalinus* (Hyaline Grass Bug, shown here) varies in color from black to yellow. Its main food is daisies.

Order: Hemiptera
Family: Rhopalidae
NA species: 36
World species: 150
Body length: 1/4–1/2 ins

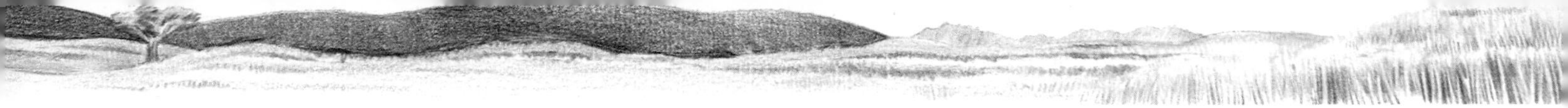

Damsel Bugs

These bugs are to be found in a wide range of habitats, from the ground to vegetation of all kinds, as long as small insects are available as prey. They catch and suck out aphids, caterpillars, and many kinds of soft-bodied insects. You may find some by sweep-netting dry grassland such as hay fields. Do not handle roughly as some members of this family can give you a painful bite. They are useful to humans because they help to control natural insect populations which include pest species.

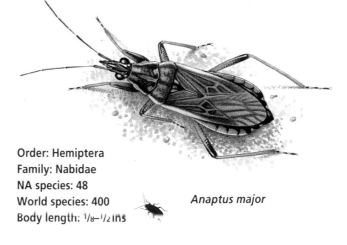

Order: Hemiptera
Family: Nabidae
NA species: 48
World species: 400
Body length: 1/8–1/2 ins

Anaptus major

Froghoppers

Adult froghoppers are active jumpers, like the spittle bugs (see opposite.) Many species are pests and can damage plants by their feeding activities. Their habitat is meadows, scrub, and woodland, all with plenty of vegetation. Their nymphs suck sap from plant stems, which produces a frothy foam. This protects them from some predators and also prevents evaporation. *Cercopis vulnerata* (shown here) is a good example of the warning colors which tell any enemy it is dangerous to eat.
Order: Hemiptera
Family: Cercopidae
NA species: 33
World species: 1,400
Body length: 1/4–3/4 ins

Seed Bugs

These are usually to be found in leaf-litter, under stones, or in low-growing vegetation such as stinging nettles. Most of the family are seed-eaters, who use their strong and spined front legs to grasp their food. Some are plant-sap suckers and a few are hunters of other insects. They produce sounds which may help to attract a mate. They use well-developed scent glands to protect themselves against enemies. Many species are pests to garden and farm crops and cause great damage. *Blissus leucopterus* (the Cinch Bug) does enormous damage to corn, wheat, rye, oats, barley, and other grain crops in North America.

Order: Hemiptera
Family: Lygaeidae
NA species: 300
World species: 3,500
Body length: 1/8–3/4 ins

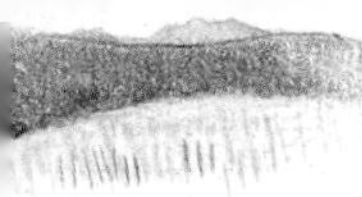

Grasslands

Mantids

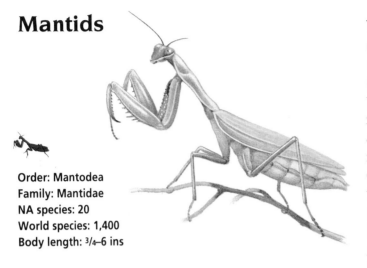

Order: Mantodea
Family: Mantidae
NA species: 20
World species: 1,400
Body length: 3/4–6 ins

These insects hold their front legs in an attitude of prayer, which is how they got their name "praying mantids." But they are simply waiting to seize any passing insects with their spiked legs. They are probably the only insects that can look over their shoulders. Their habitat is almost anywhere that has a regular supply of insect prey. They are able to snatch flying insects out of the air. *Mantis religiosa* (the European Mantid, shown here) was introduced to North America at the turn of this century. It is now common in many parts of the country. If handled, it tries to bite, but is not dangerous. A female lays a couple of hundred eggs, contained in an egg case called an "ootheca," which is attached to a plant.

Short-horned Grasshoppers & Locusts

Their common name describes their short antennae. They are found on the ground and on plants in meadows, hedges, and many other similar places in summer time, and are plant-eaters. If you walk slowly through a field on a sunny summer day, you will hear them chirping. They sing by rubbing a row of small pegs on the inside of their hind legs against the hard edge of the front wings. The Desert Locust, one of the most damaging pests in the world, belongs to this family. A very large group of shorthorned grasshoppers in North America is *Melanoplus*. There are around 300 species in this genus.

Order: Orthoptera
Family: Acrididae
NA species: 550
World species: 9,000
Body length: 1/3–3 1/8 ins

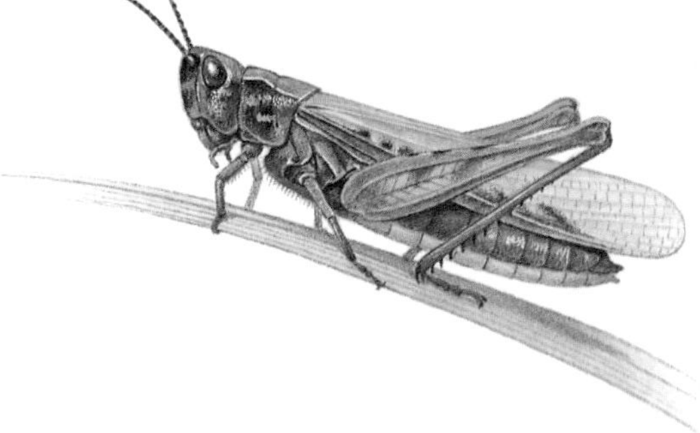

Chorthippus brunneus
(Field Grasshopper)

Stem Sawflies

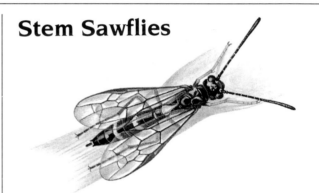

Like all sawflies, the females in this family have an ovipositor (egg laying tube), which is modified as a saw. They literally saw into plant stems to make a slit in which to lay their eggs. Their larvae look very much like the caterpillars of moths or butterflies, and burrow inside the stems of grasses, willows and other plants. Unlike other sawfly larvae, their legs are very small indeed. Look for the slow-flying adults around yellow flowers. *Cephus pygmaeus* (the Wheat Stem Sawfly, shown here) is a pest of cereal crops. Although it looks a little like a wasp, a closer look shows it has no "waist."

Order: Hymenoptera – Family: Cephidae
NA species: 12 – World species: 100 – Body length: 1/8–3/4 ins

Milkweed Butterflies

The name "milkweed" refers to the food-plant of this butterfly's caterpillars. *Danaus plexippus* (the American Monarch Butterfly, shown here) occasionally reaches European shores. It is an amazing migration for so delicate a creature, but they regularly travel from Canada to California and Mexico, where vast numbers assemble and roost. Their bright colors are a warning that they taste nasty, so birds leave them alone as a result.

Order: Lepidoptera
Family: Danaidae
NA species: 4
World species: 300
Wingspan: 2¹⁄₃–4 ins

Skippers

Thymelicus lineola
(European Skipper)

This family name refers to their active, rapid and darting flight patterns – they almost "skip" from flower to flower. You will find them in habitats where their caterpillars' food-plants grow. Although these are mainly grasses, some species like the Dingy Skipper, are found on birdsfoot trefoil and other plants. Unlike other butterfly caterpillars, this family lives within a shelter of silk-tied or rolled leaves. The caterpillars pupate at the plant's base within a silken web. You should search for skippers on a sunny day in meadows, rough grasslands, woods, and hay fields.

Order: Lepidoptera – Family: Hesperiidae
NA species: 300 – World species: 3,500 – Wingspan: ¹⁄₈–2¹⁄₂ ins

Swallowtails

This family includes the very large bird-wing butterflies of southeast Asia, the largest butterflies in the world. Swallowtails are perhaps the loveliest of all butterflies. They are beautifully marked with yellow, orange, red, green, or blue. Their caterpillars feed on many plants, including angelica, fennel, and wild carrot.

Apollo butterflies do not have hind wing tails and are white or gray in color. They are found in high places in North America and Europe. Many of these families are protected by the law in parts of the world. However, it is even more important to protect their habitats, or they will become extinct.

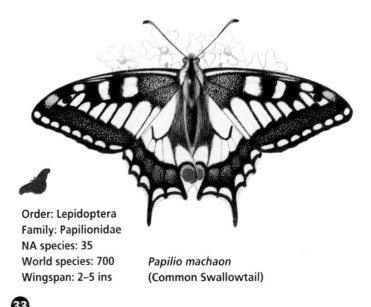

Order: Lepidoptera
Family: Papilionidae
NA species: 35
World species: 700
Wingspan: 2–5 ins

Papilio machaon
(Common Swallowtail)

Attracting Insects

A yard makes a very good nature reserve for insects. Even in the smallest town backyard you can find hundreds of different kinds. A yard contains plenty of things for insects to feed on and lots of places to hide. See how many different insects you can find in your garden. If you enjoy watching them, it is easy to encourage even more to visit your yard or window box.

Insect favorites

Butterflies, bees, and other flying insects visit flowers to feed on their sweet nectar. Buddleia, thistles, and other purple flowers are especially popular. In fact, buddleia is such a favorite with butterflies like Red Admirals that it is nicknamed the "Butterfly bush."

A wild corner

Why not ask if you can leave a small area of the backyard to grow wild? You could also scatter some wild flower seeds in your wild patch. You can buy packets of wild flower seeds at your local garden center. Don't dig up wild plants from the wild.

The wild plants that you grow there will encourage all sorts of interesting insects to move in. Nettles provide food for caterpillars, while dandelions, daisies, and buttercups attract bees and butterflies by offering them nectar to sip. In return, the insects help the flowers to reproduce.

Bees' homes

To attract solitary bees to your backyard, you could make some bee nesting burrows, using a can, some large drinking straws, and a piece of wire.

1 **Find a clean, empty can and a handful of large drinking straws.** If the straws are longer than the can, ask an adult to cut off the ends so that they are all 1 inch shorter than the can. This will keep the rain out.

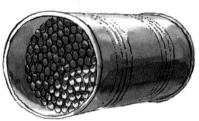

2 **Fill the can with enough straws** so that they cannot move around inside.

Moth feast

You can encourage nighttime insects such as moths by making them a tasty feast. All you will need is some brown sugar, some mushy, overripe bananas or pears, a little dark beer, a mixing bowl, and a paintbrush.

1 **Put 1 lb of brown sugar** into a mixing bowl and add one or two mushy bananas or pears. Add a little dark beer and stir the mixture well.

2 **At dusk go into the yard** with your mixture and a paintbrush. Paint some strips about 2 inches wide and 18 inches long onto the bark of a few trees.

3 **Wait patiently** for your hungry visitors to arrive.

4 **Take a small flashlight** with you. It will help you to watch the insects when it gets dark.

3 **Take the piece of wire and wind it** around the middle of the can. Fasten it so that you have enough wire left to hang the can up.

Making a pond

One of the most interesting ways to attract dragonflies is to make a pond. This is quite simple to do, and it also makes a perfect habitat for Water Boatmen and Water Beetles.

1 **Decide where you want to put the pond**. Check with an adult before making a final decision.
2 **Ask an adult to help you dig a hollow** about 18 inches deep, using a garden spade.
3 **Buy a sheet of plastic pond lining** from your local garden center. It must be big enough to fill the hole and spread out over the edge of the pond by a few inches.

4 **Now ask an adult to help you fix the bee home** under the roof of the yard shed, or on a post or tree.
5 **Watch from a distance.** In a few days you should see some bees making their nests inside. Remember bees can sting you!
6 **To make an even simpler bee home,** find a rotten log and ask an adult to drill lots of holes in it for you. Place the log on a wall, or fix it to the shed, and wait for the bees to arrive.

4 **Put some soil in the bottom of the pond** and around the edges to cover the top of the plastic lining and keep it in position.
5 **To plant your pond** you will need one or two pond plants in pots and some pond weed (like Water Milfoil). Ask your garden center for advice on what to plant.

Make a mini pond

If you don't have a backyard, or if your yard is too small for a pond, why not make a mini pond? Simply fill a large, old, plastic bowl with water and a few small water plants, then wait and see what happens.

6 **Secure the plant pots with stones** so that they don't move about, then fill the pond with water.
7 **It may take several months,** or even a year before insects begin to appear in your pond, but it's worth being patient. However, you may see midge and mosquito larvae within a few days in warm weather.

Woods & Forests

This habitat includes forests, woodland margins, and clearings. Forests are very large areas dominated by trees, which can be coniferous (trees with needles), mostly in the West, or deciduous (trees that lose their leaves in fall, like oaks or chestnuts), mostly found in the East.

Woodlands are often small patches left over from the ancient forest that may have once existed in the area. The environment inside a wood or forest is sheltered from winds and is cool and damp. In winter it stays fairly frost-free and all kinds of wildlife can find shelter among the trees throughout the year. Deciduous woods in spring, before the trees grow leaves, may have quite a few flowers. You will find bees and many other insects visiting these flowers for pollen and nectar.

Mature woods and forests with lots of different trees and with sunny clearings are the very best places for you to find insects. You should search for them in every part of a tree; the leaves, roots, bark, wood, flowers, fruit, and so on. Did you know, for instance, that an average oak tree provides a living and home for more than 300 animal species? The majority of these are insects.

As you explore a wood, look out especially for strange growths on leaves, buds, and bark. These are formed by gall wasps. Search through leaf litter as well and you will find many other specialized insects. This picture shows eleven species from this section; see how many can you identify.

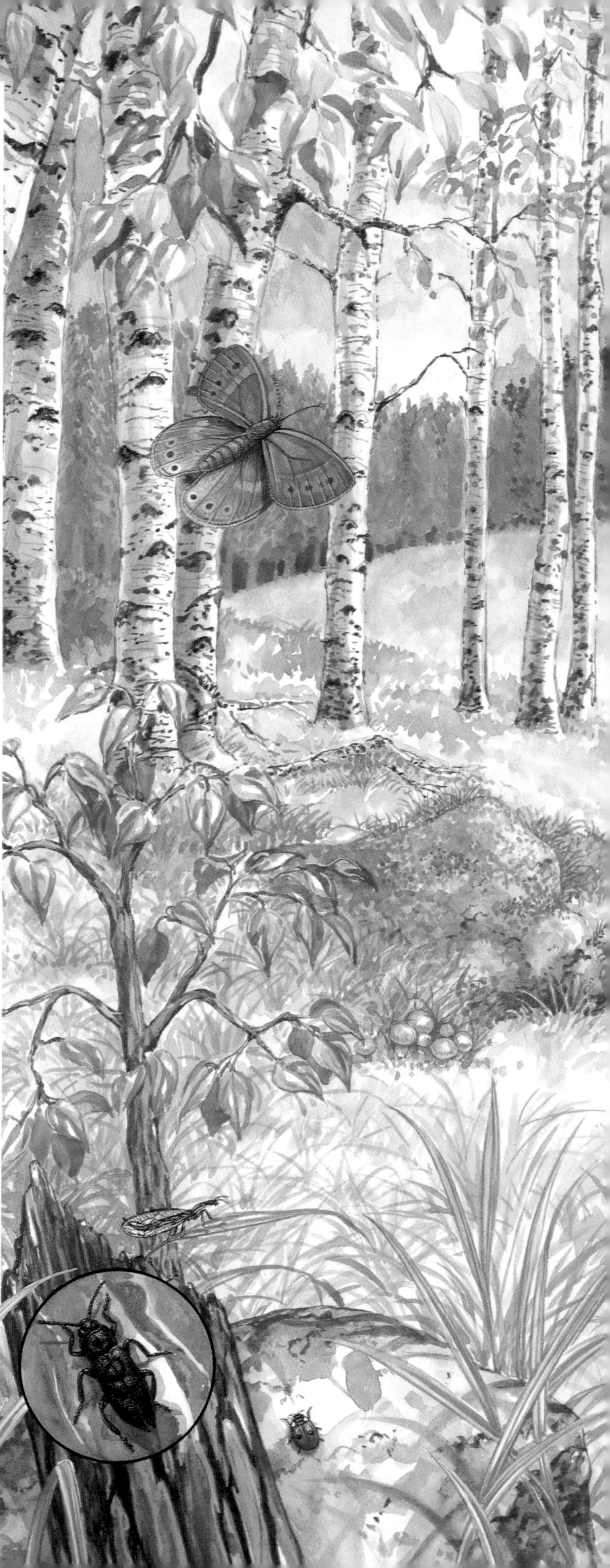

Bark Beetle, Pleasing Fungus Beetle, Jewel Beetle, Ringlet Butterfly, Glowworm, Green Lacewing, Horntail, Ladybug, Gypsy Moth, Snakefly, Termite.

Woods & Forests

Bark or Engraver Beetles

Polygraphus poligraphus

Members of this family are found in close association with many coniferous and deciduous tree species. Bark beetles have been responsible for changing the appearance of the countryside. The larvae of some species spread Dutch Elm Disease by carrying a fungus infection which clogs the sap channels of the tree and kills it. You may find the signs of these beetles if you peel back the bark of fallen or dead trees (see page 47.) Many species produce chemical attraction odors called "pheromones;" these attract many other beetles, and so cause a huge infection of the tree.

Order: Coleoptera – Family: Scolytidae
NA species: 500 – World species: 9,000 – Body length: 1/16–1/3 ins

Metallic Wood-boring Beetles

Melanophila acuminata

This family includes many of the most beautiful beetles in the world. They look a little like Click Beetles (see page 76,) but do not "jump." They are found in coniferous and deciduous woods. Female jewel beetles lay eggs in wood, and the larvae chew tunnels in the roots and trunks of trees. Some species are leaf-miners, and some bore into plant stems. Biologists have evidence that these beetles possess infra-red detectors to locate burned areas where some lay their eggs. They react to disturbance by flying off, or by pretending to be dead.

Order: Coleoptera – Family: Buprestidae – NA species: 675
World species: 14,000 – Body length: 1/16–2 1/2 ins

Death-watch Beetles

These are small, hairy, light brown or black beetles. Most measure about 1/8–1/4 ins long. Some species produce larvae which bore into wood, so they are known as woodworms. Their habitat is all kinds of wooden structures, either indoors or outside. The adult of some species attracts a mate by tapping its head against the walls of the tunnel inside the timber. These faint sounds can be heard in a quiet room. Others attack stored tobacco, spices, and drugs. *Anobium punctatum* (the Furniture Beetle, shown here) is present in many old houses.

Order: Coleoptera
Family: Anobiidae
NA species: 300
World species: 1,500
Body length: 1/16–1/3 ins

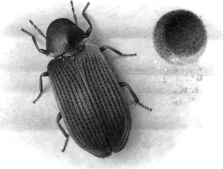

Horse & Deer Flies

Species of this family are also known as gad flies, clegs, stouts, and deer flies. The large, flattened head and large eyes are distinctive. The adult blood-sucking females will be found around mammals. They approach their prey with great stealth and alight on hard-to-reach places. Using their blade-like mouthparts, they cut into the skin and feed on the blood. The males can be seen feeding on flower nectar. The eggs are laid on plants and trees near water. The bite of these flies can cause painful swellings and even allergic reactions.

Order: Diptera
Family: Tabanidae
NA species: 350
World species: 4,100
Body length: 1/16–1 1/8 ins

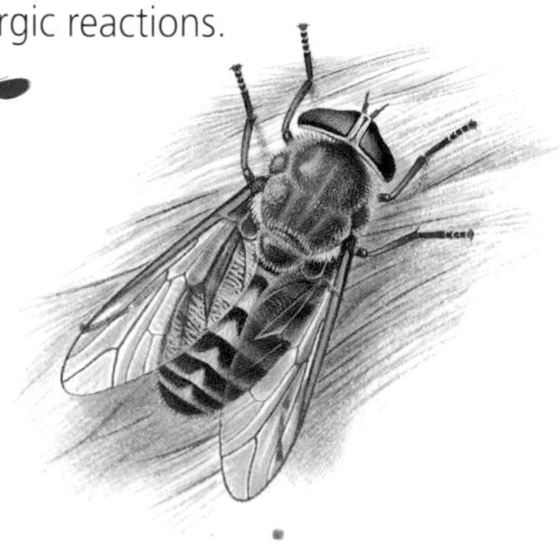

Tabanus bovinus

Tussock Moths

These beautifully marked moths have no proboscis, so they do not feed. Both adults and their caterpillars have body hairs that can give you a severe skin rash. The caterpillars drop these irritating hairs all over their pupae to protect them. They are found in hedgerows, conifer and broad-leaf woodland, and hop fields. *Lymantria dispar* (the Gypsy Moth, shown here) and the Brown-Tail Moth are two serious pest species on many trees, and both have been introduced to North America from Europe.

Order: Lepidoptera
Family: Lymantriidae
NA species: 35
World species: 2,600
Wingspan: 3/4–2 1/3 ins

Snakeflies

Their name comes from the way they resemble a snake when they hold their heads up. The long "neck" is a feature of these insects, which are to be found from May to July in thickly wooded areas. The females have a long, thin ovipositor, which is easy to see. This is used to place eggs into openings in bark, and the larvae live under loose bark. Both adults and larvae are predators on aphids (see page 16), and other small, soft-bodied insects.

Order: Megaloptera – Family: Raphidiidae
NA species: 18 – World species: 85 – Body length: 1/4–1 1/8 ins

Raphidia xanthostigma

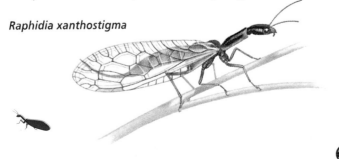

Conifer Sawflies

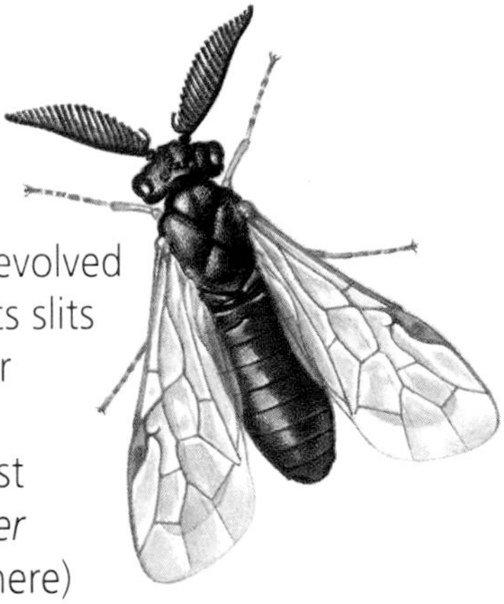

As in all sawflies, the ovipositor (egg-laying tube) in this family has evolved into a saw. With this the female cuts slits in leaves or stems and there lays her eggs. Conifer sawflies are found in conifer woods and plantations. Most species, including *Neodiprion sertifer* (the European Pine Sawfly, shown here) attack pine trees. A few prefer hemlock, firs, and spruce. Their larvae feed on the needles of the host tree. Through defoliation they kill or weaken the tree. The larvae pupate in a tough, brownish cocoon either in the soil, or glued to a twig or bark crevice.

Order: Hymenoptera – Family: Diprionidae – NA species: 41
World species: 100 – Body length: 1/4–1/2 ins

Horntails

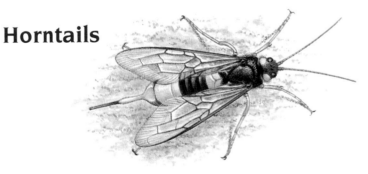

The spine or horn at the rear of the body gives this family its common name. Below this spine the female has a long ovipositor, which drills through the tree's bark and then a single egg is laid. The female *Urocerus gigas* (shown here) drills into the bark of conifers, especially firs and pines, to lay her eggs. Development may take two or more years. Males are much less easy to find, and normally fly much higher in the tree canopies. If you see a horntail, do not be alarmed—it does not sting. Species in the genera *Sirex* and *Urocerus* are widespread across the northern hemisphere.

Order: Hymenoptera – Family: Siricidae – NA species: 20
World species: 100 – Body length: 3/4–1 1/2 ins

Woods & Forests

Narrow Barklice

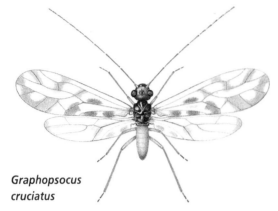

*Graphopsocus
cruciatus*

These are small, soft-bodied insects whose habitat is the underside of leaves, twigs, and branches of deciduous trees. Many prefer holly, box, and rhododendron. They lay their eggs in groups of 5–10 on stems, leaves, and fruit. These eggs are sometimes parasitized by fairyflies (see page 70.) It seems incredible to think that a minute wasp less than 1/8 ins long is able to find tiny eggs laid by a fly less than 1/16 ins long. *Graphopsocus cruciatus* (shown here) is the only narrow barklouse found in North America.

Order: Psocoptera – Family: Stenopsocidae
NA species: 1 – World species: 45 – Body length: 1/16–1/4 ins

Cicadas

The bugs in this family are well known for their songs, which are easy to hear. Each species has its own song. The songs are produced by a pair of drum-like organs called "tymbals," one each side of the abdomen near the thorax. A muscle is attached to the tymbal. Each time it contracts or relaxes, a series of sharp clicks is produced. The muscle contracts and relaxes very rapidly to make the song. The nymphs live underground, molt many times, and may take from four to seventeen years to become adults because of their poor diet of root sap. The nymphs of a well-known species in North America, *Magicicada septemdecim* (the Periodic Cicada, shown here,) construct peculiar earth chimneys above ground. In these they complete their final molt.

Order: Hemiptera
Family: Cicadidae
NA species: 166
World species: 2,500
Body length: 1–2 1/8 ins

Gall Wasps

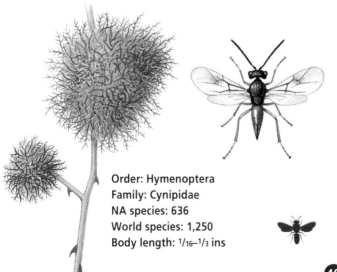

Order: Hymenoptera
Family: Cynipidae
NA species: 636
World species: 1,250
Body length: 1/16–1/3 ins

These small wasps lay their eggs inside plant tissue, then the plant produces an unusual growth called a gall. The larvae feed and grow within the gall, which protects and nourishes them. If you search in September along a hedgerow for wild roses, you will see one of the most attractive galls caused by *Diplolepis rosae* (shown here.) The gall, called a Robin's Pincushion, is like a fluffy ball of red moss. The best place to look is on the foliage and twigs of oak trees. There you will find oak-apple galls and other peculiarly shaped galls.

Fireflies or Lightningbugs

An example of this family is *Lampyris noctiluca* (shown here.) The female has no wings and emits a bright green light on the end of her body. After dark its purpose is to attract flying males to come and mate. Each species has its own flashing signal. The beetles are able to control the amount of oxygen supply to the special light organs, where a chemical reaction produces a cold, greenish light. Look out for them in spring and early summer. The larvae of some species feed on snails.

Order: Coleoptera
Family: Lampyridae
NA species: 128
World species: 2,000
Body length: 1/4–1 ins

Heleomyzid Flies

They prefer shady, moist places, like thickets and overgrown woodland, but some have been found in mammal burrows, bird's nests, and bat caves. Their larvae generally feed on decaying plants, dung, animal corpses, fungi, and seaweeds. *Heleomyza serrata* (shown here) is a typical species. Most of the genera recorded in North America occur across the northern hemisphere. However, little is known about the biology of many species in the family.

Order: Diptera
Family: Heleomyzidae
NA species: 115
World species: 500
Body length: 1/16–1/3 ins

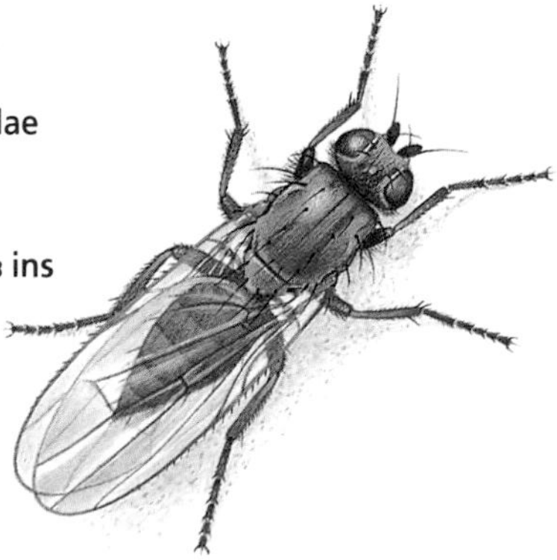

Leaf Blotch-mining Moths

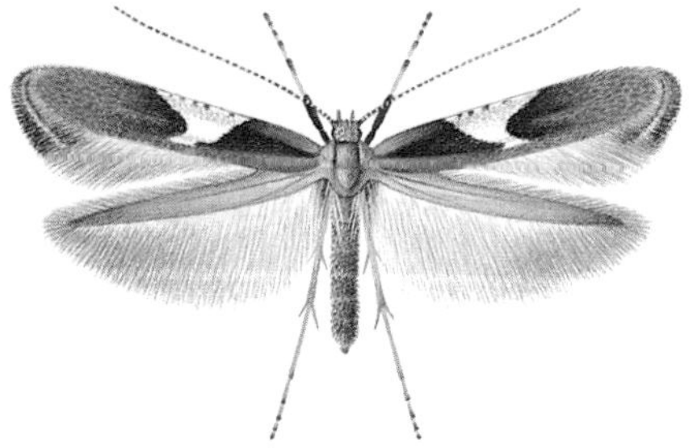

The caterpillars of these leaf-mining moths find a home between the upper and lower surfaces of leaves. In this small space they feed on the leaf tissue and so enlarge the space to form winding galleries, or blotch-like patches. Search for their "tracks" in leaves. You may discover *Caloptilia stigmatella* (the Common Lilac Leaf-miner, shown here) in a backyard, and some species are very common on oak trees. Look also for leaves which have the edges rolled; inside this kind of rainproof tent you may find some caterpillars of the family. The adults fly at dawn and dusk, and rest by day on tree trunks.

Order: Lepidoptera – Family: Gracillariidae – NA species: 280
World species: 1,200 – Wingspan: 1/8–3/4 ins

Common Scorpionflies

Their common name is obvious if you look at the end of the male's abdomen, which looks almost exactly like a scorpion's sting. Actually, it is the part of the male's reproductive system that engages with the female during mating. The head has a beak-like extension which is armed with biting mouthparts used to seize and eat dead or dying insects. Some species rob spider webs of freshly caught prey. Look for these insects on low-growing vegetation in shady places such as woodland margins. All the species occurring in North America belong to the genus *Panorpa*.

Panorpa communis

Order: Mecoptera
Family: Panorpidae
NA species: 40
World species: 360
Body length: 1/3–1 ins

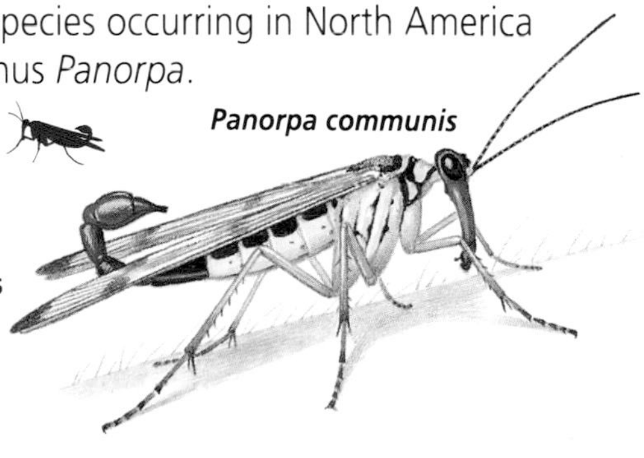

41

Long-horned Beetles

Search for these attractive beetles, sometimes called timber beetles, on flowers in a variety of habitats. Nocturnal species hide during the day under litter debris or bark. Many species are cryptically colored and others display warning colors to warn off predators. Most of them have long, narrow bodies. Their antennae are long, mostly two-thirds to four times as long as the body. Their larvae burrow into timber. Some have been known to emerge from furniture made from attacked timber. The genus *Saperda* contains several species that damage apple, poplar, and elm trees.

Order: Coleoptera
Family: Cerambycidae
NA species: 960
World species: 25,000
Body length:
1/8–7 1/8 ins

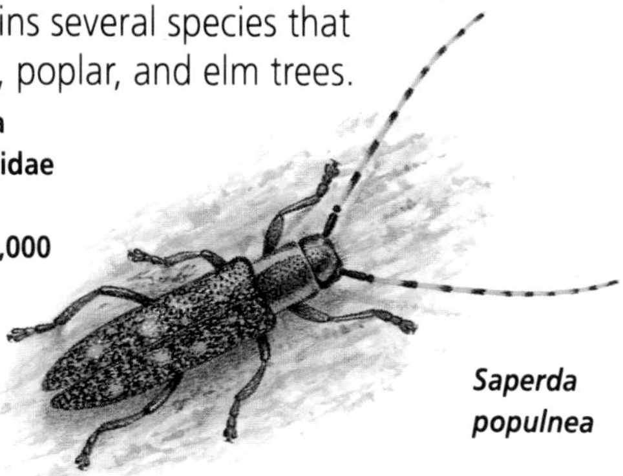

Saperda populnea

Common Barklice

If you want to find these little insects, you will have to search very thoroughly on and beneath the bark of trees, and also on twigs and branches. If you are lucky, you may encounter a herd of many hundreds, even thousands, on tree bark. They glue their eggs into crevices in the bark and cover them with a crusty layer or even silk. There are many species still awaiting discovery and description. Members of this family are very diverse and abundant in North America.

Order: Psocoptera
Family: Psocidae
NA species: 62
World species: 500
Body length: 1/16–1/4 ins

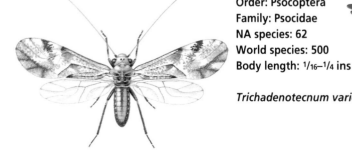

Trichadenotecnum variegatum

Lace Bugs

These small bugs are really beautiful. To appreciate the lace-like patterns you will have to take a close-up look with your hand-lens. Their habitat is the underside of leaves, especially the foliage of trees and flowers in the backyard border. Other species live on thistles and rhododendrons. A few species are attended by ants, while others make galls on their host plant. The females of some species guard their eggs, recognize their own young, and even lead the young nymphs from leaf to leaf.

Order: Hemiptera
Family: Tingidae
NA species: 160
World species: 1,820
Body length: 1/16–1/4 ins

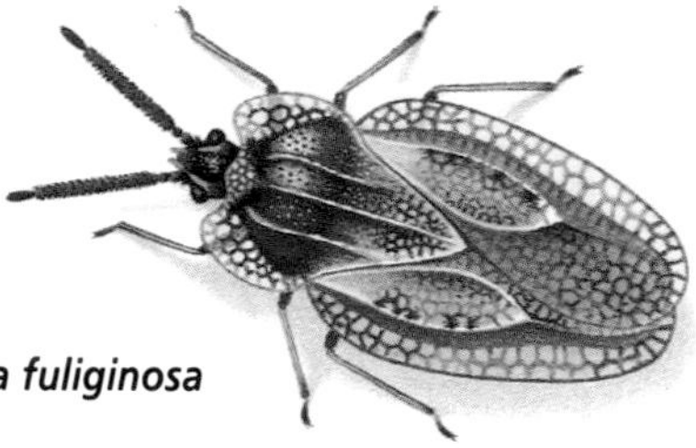

Dictyonota fuliginosa

Subterranean or Damp-wood Termites

Species of this family are found only in warmer regions. Their nests are found in damp soil or damp timbers, and they are pests because they feed on wood and can thus damage buildings. They are social insects, living in colonies of thousands of individuals, divided into workers and soldiers, each with separate functions. Despite the damage they cause, they are vital in the recycling of nutrients and an important link in ecosystems. In North America *Reticulitermes flavipes* (shown here) is widespread, and is the most destructive of all termite species.

Order: Isoptera
Family: Rhinotermitidae
NA species: 9
World species: 200
Body length: 1/4–1/3 ins

Carpenter & Leopard Moths

The Leopard Moth (*Zeuzera pyrina*, shown here) was introduced to North America from Europe. These moths live in broad-leaf forests, and their larvae are found on oak, poplar, chestnut, and willow trees. The adult lays her eggs on the bark, and the larvae feed internally in the wood. Fully-grown larvae pupate in their tunnels, or in the earth in a cocoon made of silk and chewed wood fibers.

Order: Lepidoptera – Family: Cossidae – NA species: 45
World species: 1,000 – Wingspan: 3/4–3 ins

Lappet Moths & Tent Caterpillars

Malacosoma americana, the Eastern Tent Caterpillar, is a pest on apple and wild cherry trees. It is very similar to *Malacosoma neustria (the* European Lackey Moth, shown here.) Be careful how you handle caterpillars of this family because their hairs can cause skin irritation. Some live communally in silk tents or webs spun over foliage. The fully grown caterpillars spin tough, papery, egg-shaped cocoons. You may find some of these moths flying at night, although many fly by day.

Order: Lepidoptera
Family: Lasiocampidae
NA species: 35
World species: 1,500
Wingspan: Up to 4 ins

Casebearing Moths

The caterpillars of this family feed on a range of trees, shrubs, and plants in woodlands and damp meadows. As they grow, each makes itself a case from bits of its host plant, held together with silk. The adult moths lay their eggs in summer, and the caterpillars spend the winter inside their cases. Several species are pests on apple and other fruit trees, birch, larch, and other commercial trees, like the *Coleophora serratella* (the Cigar Casebearer, shown here.)

Order: Lepidoptera
Family: Coleophoridae
NA species: 168
World species: 800
Wingspan: 1/4–1/2 ins

Long-horned Grasshoppers

Members of this family can be found from ground level to the tree tops. They are active between dusk and dawn, when you may hear the males "singing." They are also known as katydids, because their song sounds like "KATY-DID, KATY-DIDN'T." You can recognize a female by its deep and sickle-shaped ovipositor (egg-laying tube).They have hearing organs on their front legs near the knee. These insects are mainly plant-feeders but some will eat other insects. Many species can be very destructive to shrubs, trees, and crop plants.

Order: Orthoptera
Family: Tettigoniidae
NA species: 243
World species: 5,000
Body length: 2/3–3 ins

Metrioptera roeselli

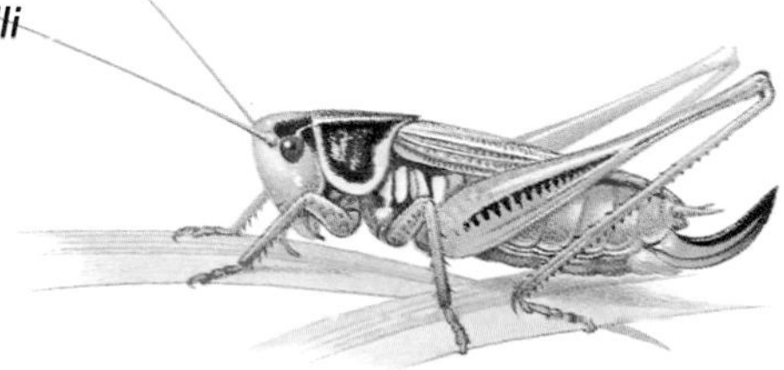

Woods & Forests

Stag Beetles

The common name of these large, shiny, black or reddish-brown insects refers to the huge jaws of the male, which look a bit like antlers. They are used for fighting during courtship. They are designed to seize the rival and flip it upside-down. Their habitat is wooded areas or along sandy beaches. They fly by night. The larvae live for up to four years in decaying tree stumps.

Lucanus cervus is very similar to the common North American species, *Lucanus elaphus*.

Order: Coleoptera
Family: Lucanidae
NA species: 32
World species: 1,250
Body length: 1/4–3 1/3 ins

Pleasing Fungus Beetles

These small to medium-sized, oval, shiny beetles have a metallic sheen. Where tree bark is damaged and sap is flowing down the trunk, they move in to a rich source of food. Most lay eggs on fungi, and the larvae burrow deep within to feed on the fruiting bodies of the larger fungi. If you come across some fungus-infected, rotting wood, look a little closer—there may be some of this family about. Some species feed on bracket fungi, which usually grow on wood. They are a good example of how insects have adapted to a wide variety of food sources.

Order: Coleoptera
Family: Erotylidae
NA species: 65
World species: 2,000
Body length: 1/8–1 ins

Dacne bipustulata

Ladybug Beetles

Ladybugs, or ladybirds, come in a variety of colors and number of spots. The background of the wing-case can be black, red, yellow, or orange. The number of spots can vary from two to twenty-four. They are found in a wide range of habitats, as long as suitable food is available. The adults of most species feed on aphids and soft-bodied insects. Their larvae also eat vast numbers of aphids (see page 16). In addition to their warning colors, ladybirds give out a yellow fluid from their leg joints, which makes them taste nasty.

Order: Coleoptera
Family: Coccinellidae
NA species: 400
World species: 5,000
Body length: 1/16–1/3 ins

Adalia bipunctata

Brown Lacewings

Micromus angulatus

A family of carnivorous insects found in deciduous woodland, backyards, and hedgerows. One brown lacewing may eat many thousands of aphids, mealy bugs, and scale insects. They are therefore very effective in reducing natural populations of some pests. The best time to look for them is when they become active from dusk onward. They produce several broods in a year.

Order: Neuroptera – Family: Hemerobiidae
NA species: 58 – World species: 900 – Body length: 1/8–1/2 ins

Atlas, Emperor, Moon, & Royal Butterflies

These large, heavy-bodied moths are often brightly colored. The best examples are found in the South of the U.S., and in the tropics where the largest can grow to a wingspan of 8 ins across. Most species have an "eyespot" near the center of each wing. The adults cannot feed as they do not have proper mouth parts. Their caterpillars are covered in fleshy knobs that carry spines and long, bristly hairs. The species shown (*Samia cynthia*) was introduced to North America from Europe.

Order: Lepidoptera
Family: Saturniidae
NA species: 69
World species: 1,100
Wingspan: 1–6 ins

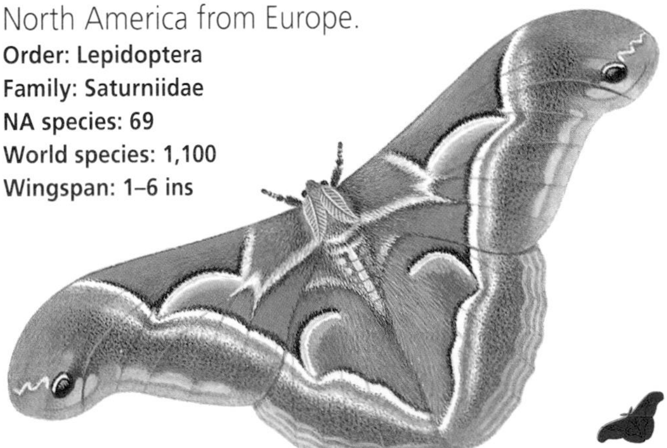

Fungus Gnats

These are mosquito-like flies favoring moist, woody areas, but they are also found in houses. Look for the long legs and humped thorax, like the adult *Mycetophila fungorum* (shown here,) and adults on the wing between March and August. The worm-like, whitish larvae of some species feed in dung, rotting wood, and other plant matter. Others feed on woody bracket fungi, or fleshy fungi. In some parts of the world, cave-living species lure other small insects into silken threads. Various species are a serious pest to cultivated mushrooms.

Order: Diptera
Family: Mycetophilidae
NA species: 720
World species: 3,000
Body length: 1/16–1/2 ins

Arctic, Nymph, & Satyr Butterflies

This is a family of shade-lovers found in heathland, open meadows, and light woodland in upland areas. Their caterpillars all eat grass or sedges (wetland grasses,) and have a pair of points at the tail end. When on the wing, these butterflies may be recognized by their erratic and bobbing flight. The genus *Erebia* is typical of the mountains of North America. In fact, the majority of North American satyrid species are found in the north, or in the mountains of the West.

Coenonympha tullia

Order: Lepidoptera
Family: Satyridae
NA species: 50
World species: 2,000
Wingspan: 11/8–3 ins

Be an Insect Detective

Once you know where to look for insects, you can become an expert by exploring different habitats. Start by looking closely at a small habitat (a microhabitat), such as a pond, a compost heap, or even a window box, to see what lives there.

Looking at leaves and stems

Garden plants often contain evidence of all kinds of insect activity. Have a look in your garden to see what you can detect on the leaves and stems.

- Look carefully on a **blackberry bush** and you will probably find that some of the leaves are rolled up. Can you see a caterpillar inside?

- Little white lines on a **blackberry leaf** may have been caused by insects called Leaf-mining Flies (see page 15). Hold a leaf up to the light, or hold a flashlight behind it to see if you can detect the insects tunneling through it.

- If you look closely at the leaves on a **rose bush** you will probably find that some have been nibbled around the edges. This is a sign that a Leaf-cutter Bee (see page 18) has been taking away pieces of leaf to make cocoons for its eggs.

- If the **stems and buds of roses** are sticky and green, this is probably a mass of Aphids (see page 16) which suck the sap inside the plant. You may also see a Ladybug (see page 44) feeding on the aphids.

- **Froth on the stems of a plant** is evidence of a Leafhopper (see page 16), which lives inside the bubbles that are known as "cuckoo spit." See if you can find some in your backyard or park.

- **Swellings on grass stems or leaves** may contain the larvae of flies or moths. They are called "galls." Take some home and ask an adult to open them carefully with a sharp knife. Sometimes they contain a spider, ant, or thrip which has moved into the empty gall.

Mushroom homes

Fungi provide homes and food for many kinds of insects. It you look at the gills of a fully grown wild mushroom or toadstool, you may see little black specks. Look with a magnifying glass and you will see that each speck is the head of a little white larva. Break it open to see how the larvae eat tiny tunnels through the cap. **Always wash your hands** after touching fungi; **never eat** wild fungi.

A world in an oak tree

A tree like an oak is a habitat for thousands of creatures. The leaves, fruits, and seeds are food for beetles, ants, aphids, bees, wasps, moths, and many more insects, which in turn are eaten by birds and mammals. Count how many kinds of insects you see buzzing around or crawling over a single tree. You may be surprised to discover that the tree is alive with wildlife. Make a note of the insects that you see and what they are doing.

Life inside a log

All kinds of creatures burrow into rotting wood and tree bark. If you find a piece of mossy, rotting wood, take it home in a plastic container. Keep the lid on so that the insects do not escape before you have finished studying them in their home.

1 **Peel away some moss and bark** to see what is hiding there. You may find beetles, earwigs, or even a centipede. Centipedes are not insects—they have too many legs—but they often hunt small insects.

2 **Break off part of the log**, or piece of wood to see if there are burrowing insects. Holes in the wood may be woodworm, which is caused by burrowing Death-watch Beetle larvae.

3 **When you have finished** looking at your log habitat, put it outside in the yard.

Deserts & Savanna

There are two main deserts in North America, and both are in the West. The Great Basin runs through Nevada. Southwest of this, in California, is the Mojave Desert. You can easily tell when you are in a desert because the ground is very dry and over half of it is bare of plants. It may rain from time to time, but never for long.

Most desert plants survive the dry conditions by storing water in their stems or in bulbs under the ground. The best places to look for insects is near plants, or around water holes. Savanna is dry grassland with only limited amounts of rain. This picture shows eight species from this section; see how many can you identify.

Ant Lion, Velvet Ant, Digger Bee, Tiger Beetle, Robber Fly, Solitary Wasp, Spider-hunting Wasp, Tiphid Wasp.

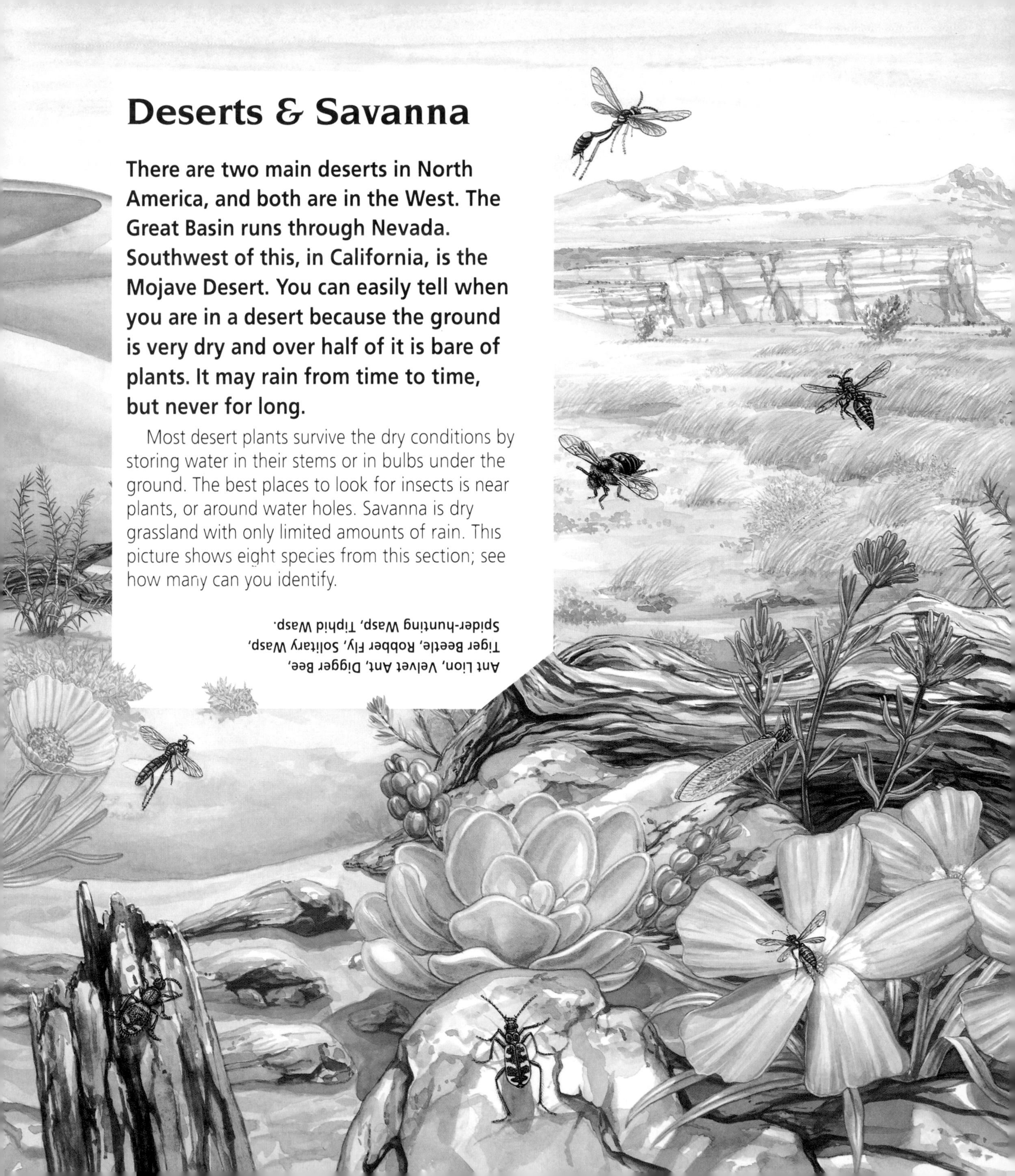

Antlions

At a quick glance these large, slender-bodied insects look like damselflies (see page 55.) But if you look more closely and carefully, you will see that Antlions have club-ended antennae. Search for them on dunes, and in warm, dry sandy places. They are called antlions because some species prey on ants. The larvae, called doodlebugs in North America, live in sand at the bottom of conical pits. When an ant arrives, the antlion larva flicks sand at it. When the ant falls into the trap, it is seized and eaten.

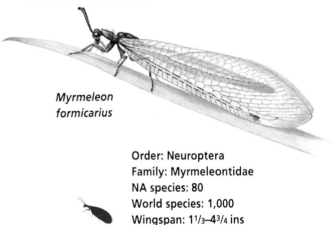

Myrmeleon formicarius

Order: Neuroptera
Family: Myrmeleontidae
NA species: 80
World species: 1,000
Wingspan: 1¹/₃–4³/₄ ins

Oil or Blister Beetles

Meloe proscarabaeus

Beware! These beetles produce fluids that can raise blisters on your skin, so look but do not touch. You may see them on flowers and low-growing foliage and grass. The larvae of many species are found in the soil and eat the eggs of grasshoppers or bees. In some species, the larva attaches itself to the body of a solitary bee visiting a flower. When the female bee lays her eggs, the beetle larva sneaks into the cell with the egg. It then eats the bee's egg and the food provisions left by the parent bee for its intended offspring.

Order: Coleoptera
Family: Meloidae
NA species: 315
World species: 2,000
Body length: ¹/₄–1¹/₃ ins

Tiger Beetles

Look for these beetles in sunny, warm, open areas, such as dry grassland and sandy places. Choose a sunny day in spring to early summer. Adult tiger beetles are fierce predators and are among the fastest insect runners. They have a top speed of 1¹/₂ mph. Their larvae dig vertical burrows, up to 11 ins deep. They wait at the top, head and jaws filling the opening, to seize any passing insect and drag it down to be eaten. Both larva and adult beetle live up to their name of Tiger Beetle. If handled carelessly, they may give you a painful bite.

Cicindela hybrida

Order: Coleoptera
Family: Cicindellidae
NA species: 108
World species: 2,000
Body length: ¹/₄–1 ins

Deserts & Savanna

Darkling Beetles

Order: Coleoptera
Family: Tenebrionidae
NA species: 1,008
World species: 15,000
Body length: $1/16$–$1^3/4$ ins

Tenebrio obscurus

Many species belonging to this interesting family are adapted to life in very dry conditions, such as deserts and grain stores. Some species produce jets of blistering chemical spray to deter their enemies, but some predatory mammals know this danger. They stick the beetle's spraying tail-end in the ground and eat them head first. Many species have very reduced hind wings, so they do not fly. Mostly they prefer to live in dark places—hence their name. Some are called flour beetles and are pests of cereals, flour, and other dried produce.

Robber or Assassin Flies

A well-named family because their mouthparts are adapted for stabbing and sucking. Most species will perch on an exposed twig or stone where they keep a look-out for a passing insect. If one flies near, the assassin fly chases it and seizes it on the wing with its strong, bristly legs. It quickly injects a nerve anaesthetic which paralyzes the prey. Some species hunt for ground-moving prey. Many of the family mimic bees and wasps, and no insect prey is too large for them. They catch and kill dragonflies, bees, and grasshoppers, as well as other insects. They are most active in warm sunshine in open or lightly wooded areas, especially if they are dry.

Order: Diptera
Family: Asilidae
NA species: 900
World species: 5,000
Body length: $1/8$–2 ins

Dioctria baumhaueri

Digger, Cuckoo, & Carpenter Bees

Anthophora furcata

Digger bees dig burrows, cuckoo bees lay eggs in the nests of other bees, and carpenter bees excavate burrows in timber. They are mainly solitary bees. Their habitat is widespread—they live wherever there are plenty of flowers. Cuckoo bees leave their young to feed on pollen and honey collected by their host. Digger bees collect a supply of honey and pollen and leave it in the larval cells.

Order: Hymenoptera
Family: Anthophoridae
NA species: 920
World species: 4,200
Body length: $1/8$–$1^1/8$ ins

Velvet Ants

Another misleading common name—these insects are velvety, but although some of them look like ants, they are not ants—they are wasps. The males of some species are found on flowers. The females are wingless, and are usually seen running over the ground in dry, shady, or open habitats. They are parasites on the larvae and pupae of many bees and wasps. Female velvet ants have incredibly powerful stings which cause intense pain—so don't pick them up. In North America the genus *Dasymutilla* contains species known as cow or mule killers, but they do not actually kill.

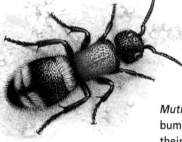

Order: Hymenoptera
Family: Mutillidae
NA species: 480
World species: 5,000
Body length: 1/8–1 ins

Mutilla europaea prefers bumble bees as food for their larvae.

Tiphiid Wasps

Adults of this family feed on flower nectar and honeydew. Females are usually seen running over the ground. They seem to prefer dry, sandy, and warm situations. All are parasitic on the larvae of beetles, bees, and wasps. The ant-like female of *Methocha* will run over the ground searching for tiger beetle larvae (see page 49) in their burrows. She has to avoid the larva's powerful jaws, paralyze it, and lay her egg. She then fills in the burrow. Some species have been investigated as possible biological control agents.

Order: Hymenoptera
Family: Tiphiidae
NA species: 225
World species: 1,500
Body length: 1/8–1 1/8 ins

Solitary Hunting, Digger, & Sand Wasps

The common names of these various sub-groups tell you their different habits. They live in sunny, sandy, open habitats. The adults feed at flowers and any source of sugary liquid. The females hunt

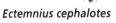

Ectemnius cephalotes

and catch insects and spiders, which they paralyze or kill. The prey is placed in the nest, which is in the ground, in rotten wood, hollow stems, or burrows of other insects. Once the nest burrow is stocked with prey and eggs are laid, the larvae will develop on the food store.

Order: Hymenoptera – Family: Sphecidae – NA species: 1,140
World species: 8,000 – Body length: 1/16–1 3/4 ins

Spider Wasps

Adults can be seen on flowers, or running over the ground in open, dry, sandy habitats. They flick and jerk their wings continuously as they run. Their venom will paralyze even the largest spider, but the wasp has to avoid the spider's venomous fangs. If successful, the wasp lays a single egg on the paralyzed spider and buries it in the sand. A few species cheat by laying an egg on another wasp's prey. Either way, the growing larva has spider-meat for a meal. Beware of these wasps; their stings are extremely painful.

Order: Hymenoptera
Family: Pompilidae
NA species: 290
World species: 4,000
Body length: 1/4–2 ins

Anoplius nigerrimus

Catching Insects

If you want to look at water insects in your pond, or insects that you cannot catch with a pooter (see page 25), why not make some simple traps for collecting live insects without harming them?

Remember to handle all insects gently while you observe them, then set them free afterward where you found them. Be extra careful not to trap insects that could sting you, such as wasps, bees, and hornets, and never try to catch delicate insects such as butterflies, moths, or dragonflies.

Make a pitfall trap

The best way to catch crawling insects like beetles is to make a pitfall trap, which you put in the ground. **You will need:** a clean jelly jar, a trowel, a large, flat stone, and four pebbles.

Make a beating tray

An easy way to look at insects that live on trees is to make a beating tray. **You will need**: two bamboo canes about 18 inches long, one bamboo cane 3 feet long, some white cloth (a piece of old sheet will do,) strong glue or a stapler, some string or wire, and a long stick.

1 **Place one of the short canes across the top of the long cane** to make a "T" shape, and secure it tightly with some string or wire.
2 **Then lay the other short cane across the middle** of the long cane and fix it with wire or string so that it cannot move around.

1 **Choose a sheltered area of the garden** and dig a small hole in the earth, just deep enough for the jelly jar.
2 **Put the jar into the hole** so that the rim is level with the ground. Make sure it doesn't wobble too much. Put a couple of leaves or a bit of grass into the jar.
3 **Put the flat stone over the top of the jar**, propped up by the pebbles to keep out the rain.
4 **Every few hours, remove the stone** and look to see if any beetles or other crawling insects have fallen into the trap. Have a look at night and in the early morning too.
5 **Remember that once an insect falls into the jar**, it cannot get out by itself, so you will have to release it.
6 **When you have finished using your pitfall trap**, remove the jar and fill in the hole.

3 **Now cut enough white cloth** to lay across the bamboo frame and overlap the edges by 2 inches all round.

4 **Lay the cloth on the ground,** then lay the frame on top. Fold the edges of the cloth over the frame and fix it with fabric glue or staples. If this is difficult, ask an adult to help you. If you glue it, don't use the tray until the glue is dry.

5 **Now find a long stick and a suitable tree**—oaks, beeches, or birches are good. Stand under the tree, holding your beating tray horizontally.

7 **Give one of the leafy branches a sharp blow.** Lots of different insects should drop onto your beating tray. You may find it easier if one person holds the tray and the other uses the stick. Be careful not to damage the tree.

Looking at water insects

Only ever visit a pond or stream with an adult, and approach quietly and carefully so that you don't disturb the water creatures. Never run, because you could easily trip and fall in.

If you want to catch pond creatures, you will need a net. You can buy one quite cheaply, or you could make your own, using a bamboo cane with an old sieve attached to one end. You also need a bucket filled with pond water.

1 **Push your net slowly through the water,** close to the edges and around the plants.

2 **Lift the net out of the water gently,** then empty it by dipping it into the bucket of water.

3 **Don't forget to put the insects back** into the pond after you have identified them.

Rivers, Bogs, & Wetlands

This habitat includes anywhere wet from marshes to lakes and the great rivers. Fresh water is in short supply (97 percent of the world's water is salt), yet it provides an amazing range of habitats.

There is a whole world in a discarded can or tire that holds a tiny "pool" of rainwater—an ideal breeding haunt for gnats and mosquitoes whose larvae are aquatic. Hollows in trees and plant leaves that trap water at their bases also provide breeding sites. On a larger scale there are rain butts, ponds, and streams.

In fast streams only those insects with devices for holding on to the bottom can survive. Slow-flowing streams and ponds will have lots of interesting insects. The picture shows twelve species from this section; how many can you identify?

Alderfly, Backswimmer, Diving Beetle, Whirligig Beetle, Shore Bug, Black Fly, Caddisfly, Damselfly, Darter, Mayfly, Stonefly, Water Strider.

Narrow-winged Damselflies

You will find this family mainly along streams and rivers, but also around ponds, brackish pools, and swampy places. Damselflies are mostly smaller than dragonflies, and have a feeble and fluttering flight. When at rest, the wings of damselflies are held together along the body, whereas in dragonflies they are held out sideways. Female narrow-winged damselflies use their ovipositors (egg-laying tubes) to make slits in submerged plants and then insert their eggs. In some cases, the female will crawl under the surface to a depth of 12 ins or more.

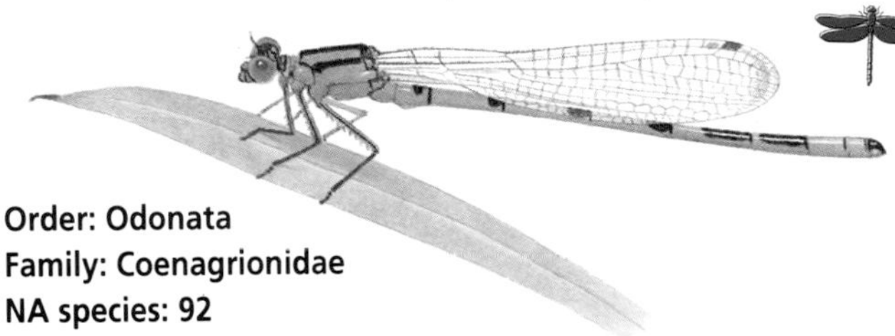

Order: Odonata
Family: Coenagrionidae
NA species: 92
World species`: 1,000
Wingspan: 3/4–13/4 ins

Enallagma cyathigerum
(Common Blue Damselfly)

Darners

This family includes some of the largest and most powerful of the world's dragonflies. They hunt on the wing and seize many kinds of insects. Search for them in areas of still water during the midsummer months. They are inquisitive insects and investigate any moving object in their territory, including you. The aquatic nymphs, like all dragonfly nymphs, are aggressive. You can catch them in your pond net if you push it through pond vegetation (see page 53.)

Order: Odonata
Family: Aeshnidae
NA species: 34
World species: 500
Wingspan: 21/8–41/3 ins

Aeshna subarctica

Spread-winged Damselflies

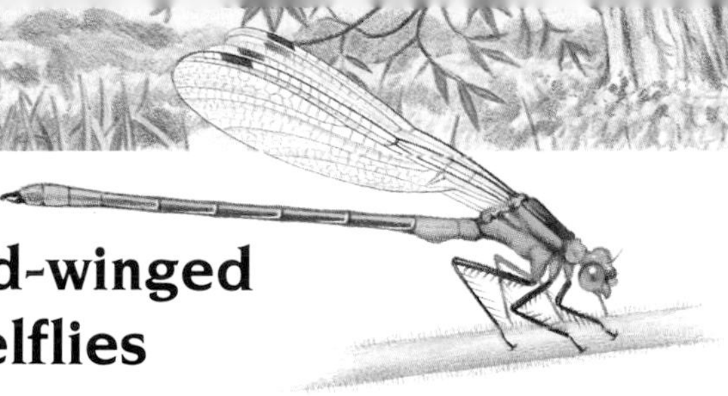

Lestes dryas

These relatively large damselflies are usually metallic blue, bronze, or green in color. Unlike members of other damselfly families, they rest with their wings slightly open and the body held vertical to the stem. On a warm, bright day between July and September you can see them sunning themselves on plants around still water, boggy areas, wet ditches, or lakes. Females lay their eggs in plant stems above water level. Larvae take about eight weeks to develop. Like all dragonfly and damselfly larvae, they have a so-called "mask" which is a part of the jaw folded back under the head. They lie in wait for a small fish or other aquatic life to come near, then the mask shoots forward and their strong claws seize the prey.

Order: Odonata – Family: Lestidae – NA species: 18
World species: 200 – Wingspan: 11/4–21/2 ins

Common Skimmers

You will see these broad-bodied dragonflies flying over still water in a variety of habitats from dense forest to arid areas. Adult males are very territorial —they will guard their patch from a high perch on an exposed stem or twig and chase off any intruder. This is something you can watch, simply by sitting quietly and observing. Eggs are laid by the female hovering over the water and dipping the tip of her abdomen below the surface. The species shown here is often found in coastal areas, but can also be found in high hilly regions.

Order: Odonata
Family: Libellulidae
NA species: 91
World species: 1,250
Wingspan: 3/4–4 ins

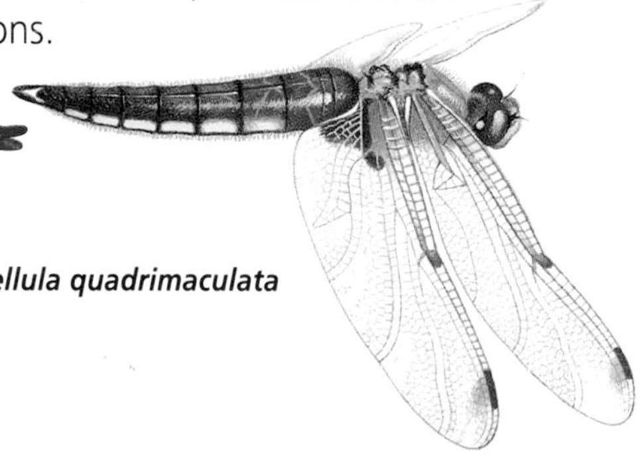

Libellula quadrimaculata

Black Flies

Simulium austeni

The females of some species of this family require a blood meal from birds, horses, and cattle before they lay their eggs. They have a stout body and a distinctive, humpbacked thorax. The males suck nectar. Their habitat is around fast-flowing water, where the eggs are laid on plants or stones both above and below water. The larvae feed by filtering tiny particles and organisms from the water. In cool parts of the northern hemisphere they do not harm humans. However, in Africa they transmit river blindness and other parasitic diseases to humans, birds, and animals.

Order: Diptera – Family: Simuliidae – NA species: 150
World species: 1,500 – Body length: 1/16–1/4 ins

Mosquitoes

You will often hear these flies before you see them, for you can tell a flying mosquito by its high-pitched whine. Although the males feed on nectar and honeydew, the females are blood-suckers. When a female alights, she feels for a soft spot on the skin, then bores through it with her mouthparts and has her meal. You should look for the egg rafts of mosquitoes floating on the surface of water butts, other rain-filled containers, and ponds. Their larvae, called "wrigglers," hatch from these eggs. Put some in a jelly jar and look at them with a hand lens, then return them to the place where you found them. In tropical countries mosquitoes are carriers of many diseases, including malaria and yellow fever.

Order: Diptera
Family: Culicidae
NA species: 150
World species 3,100
Body length: 1/8–1/3 ins

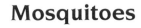

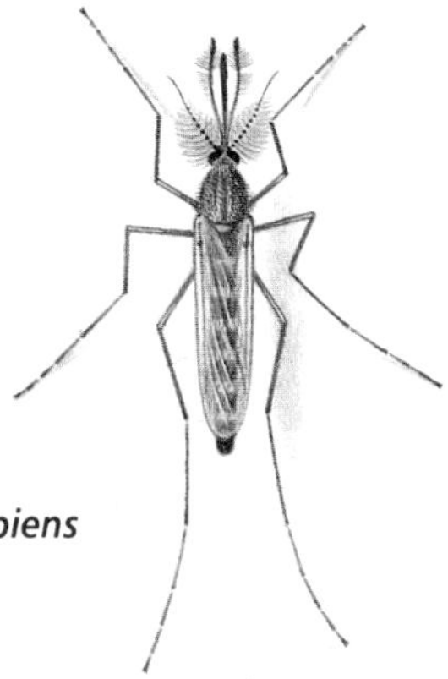

Culex pipiens

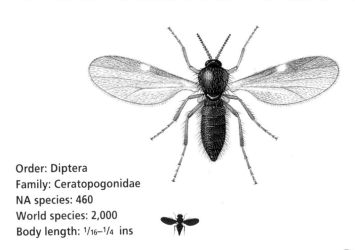

Order: Diptera
Family: Ceratopogonidae
NA species: 460
World species: 2,000
Body length: 1/16–1/4 ins

Biting Midges or Punkies

Because of their small size midges are often called "no-see-ums." But you will certainly feel the effect of their biting and blood-sucking, especially near sunset. Most species do not fly more than 100 yards from their breeding ground in moist habitats such as bogs, pond margins, rivers, lakes, and close to the seashore. Some species, like *Forcipomyia bipunctata* (shown here,) suck the body fluids of larger insects such as dragonflies, moths, and beetles; others catch and eat smaller insects.

The Ephemeroptera are the oldest group of winged insects on Earth today. The name of the order comes from two Greek words: *ephemeros* (lasting a day) and *pteron* (a wing) because the adults mostly live for less than a day.

Burrowing Mayflies

Look for the adult mayflies from mid-April to September when you may see vast numbers flying above a river or stream. The front legs of their nymphs (young stage) are adapted for digging. They burrow into sand or silt at the bottom of streams, rivers, lakes, or ponds. Their specially adapted mouthparts move the silt, which is then pushed backward by the legs. Members of this family are important links in the freshwater-fish food chains. *Ephemera danica* (shown here) is among the largest of North American mayflies. Anglers use models of it as lures, and it is known as a "Green Drake."

Order: Ephemeroptera
Family: Ephemeridae
NA species: 13
World species: 150
Body length: 1/2–1 1/4 ins

Small Mayflies

To find the nymphs (young stages) of these beautiful mayflies, try pond-dipping (see page 53) in their habitat, which is still or running water. Streams, rivers, ditches, ponds, or lakes may provide you with some specimens. If you keep some in your aquarium, be sure to plant it with a variety of aquatic plants because the nymphs are herbivorous (plant-eating.) *Cloeon dipterum* (shown here) gives birth to live nymphs and does not lay eggs. Other species of small mayflies will enter water or even go through waterfalls to lay their eggs on rocks. Some species can live in polluted water, which is unusual for most insects.

Order: Ephemeroptera
Family: Baetidae
NA species: 147
World species: 800
Body length: 1/16–1/2 ins

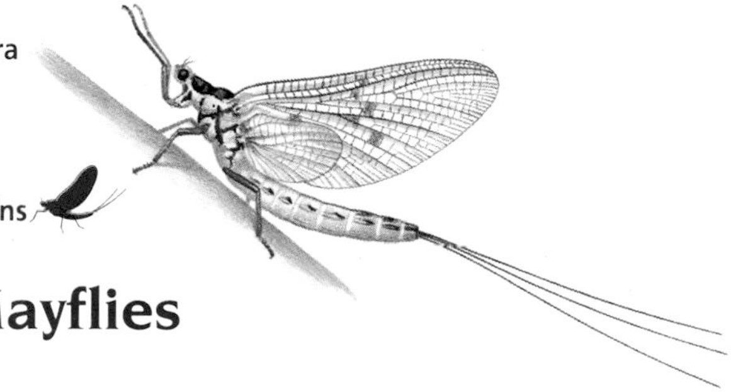

Prongill Mayflies

One way to distinguish members of this family from other mayflies is by the length of their three long tails. In prongill mayflies they are obviously longer than the body. Their habitat is slow-flowing streams and lakes. The nymphs prefer to live in crevices under stones and logs, or in plant debris. They eat plants and the debris. These nymphs are freely eaten by fish and thus form an important link in the food chain.

Order: Ephemeroptera – Family: Leptophlebiidae
NA species: 70 – World species: 600
Body length: 1/8–1/2 ins

Leptophlebia marginata

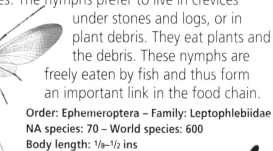

Stream Mayflies

Try pond-dipping (see page 53) for the nymphs of these mayflies in fast-running mountain streams. If you catch one, observe it in some water in a plastic dish, then return it to its habitat. They are difficult to keep in an aquarium because they are used to cold, fast-running water rich in oxygen. As they are an important freshwater fish food, anglers use models of both nymphs and adults as lures for fly fishing. The nymphs of many species are active and can move easily in all directions.

Order: Ephemeroptera – Family: Heptageniidae
NA species: 133 – World species: 550
Body length: 1/8–1/2 ins

Rhithrogena semicolorata

Perlodid Stoneflies

Some adult species of this family have no working mouthparts, so they live for less than two weeks using the food reserves within their bodies. Other species may feed on pollen. In contrast, their nymphs are carnivorous (meat-eating) or omnivorous (they eat everything.) When fully grown, they crawl out of the water, rest on a stone, and the adult emerges. They are found near cold, stony, and gravel-bottomed streams; some species live in water rich in limestone. The best time to look for the day-flying adults is from late spring to early summer. Most species are to be found in the North and West, but they are not common.

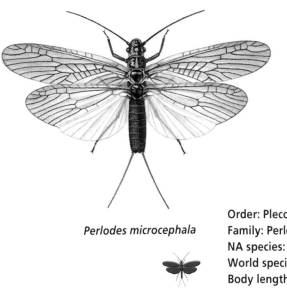

Perlodes microcephala

Order: Plecoptera
Family: Perlodidae
NA species: 98
World species: 250
Body length: 1/4–1 ins

Spring or Brown Stoneflies

Nymphs may pass through thirty molts and take four years to become adults. Their eggs may be adhesive, flattened, spindle-shaped, and with a thread-like attachment to stick to underwater objects. You should search for them in fast-flowing, rocky streams. They are weak fliers, usually in warm sunshine. Many species avoid polluted water and prefer cold, oxygen-rich water. The vast majority of the American species belong to the genus *Nemoura* (one is shown here.) This family are used as models for the anglers' flies called "Early Brown."

Nemoura cinerea

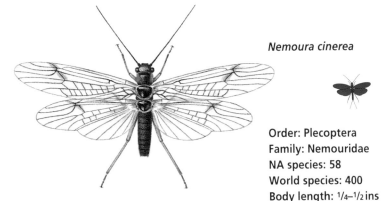

Order: Plecoptera
Family: Nemouridae
NA species: 58
World species: 400
Body length: 1/4–1/2 ins

Rolled-winged Stoneflies

Some species of this family are called needleflies because of their small size and slender shape. When at rest, the wings appear to be tightly rolled together over the sides of the body. Their favored habitat is small streams and springs, but they are also to be found beside lakes in lowlands and uplands. *Leuctra geniculata* (shown here) belongs to the largest genus in this family, which is found throughout the northern hemisphere.

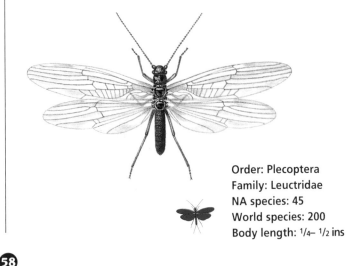

Order: Plecoptera
Family: Leuctridae
NA species: 45
World species: 200
Body length: 1/4–1/2 ins

Non-biting Midges

This is a family of gnat-like flies that look a little like mosquitoes. Look for them between April and September over trees, bushes, or water. You will often see swarms of them towards dusk "dancing" up and down in still air, and the females mating before they lay eggs on the water surface. Most of their three-year life cycle is spent under water as larvae—the adults only live a week or two. The larvae of some species of this family are often called blood worms because of their red color. A few species live on the seashore, and some even live in thermal springs.

Order: Diptera
Family: Chironomidae
NA species: 820
World species: 5,000
Body length: 1/16–1/3 ins

Chironomus plumosus

Micro Caddisflies

The smallest species of caddisflies belong to this family. Their habitat is near rivers, lakes, and ponds. Mating swarms fly over the water and lay jelly-like egg masses both on the water and marginal plants. The first four larval stages move freely in the water, sucking the juices of water plants. The last larval stage produces silk from its mouthparts and weaves an open-ended barrel or purse-shaped case. The larva pupates inside this case and emerges at the water surface.

Order: Trichoptera
Family: Hydroptilidae
NA species: 200
World species: 1,000
Body length: 1/16–1/4 ins

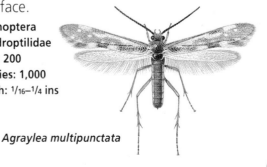

Agraylea multipunctata

Northern Caddisflies

Limnephilus rhombicus

Search for these common caddisflies around ponds, lakes, and still water. *Limnephilus rhombicus*, a typical adult caddisfly, is a member of a widespread genus of more than ninety species in North America. These species and their larvae live in cases made from tiny pieces of plant stem, stones, sand grains, and small snail shells. Some species make cases from small twigs and these are known as log cabins. Use your pond net gently and push it through the underwater plants to catch the larvae.

Order: Trichoptera – Family: Limnephilidae – NA species: 310
World species: 1,500 – Body length: 1/4–11/4 ins

Large Caddisflies

Adults' wings of some species can be brightly marked with orange and black. You will find them near ponds, lakes, marshes, and slow-moving parts of streams, and rivers. The larvae make beautiful, regular, tapering cases of spirally arranged plant fragments. The pieces of plant fragment used are cut to an exact size as the larva measures them against the front part of its body. Some cases can be up to nearly 21/2 ins long.

Order: Trichoptera
Family: Phryganeidae
NA species: 26
World species: 500
Body length: 1/2–1 ins

Agrypnia pagetana

Stilt Bugs

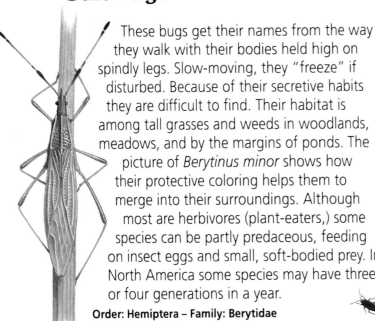

These bugs get their names from the way they walk with their bodies held high on spindly legs. Slow-moving, they "freeze" if disturbed. Because of their secretive habits they are difficult to find. Their habitat is among tall grasses and weeds in woodlands, meadows, and by the margins of ponds. The picture of *Berytinus minor* shows how their protective coloring helps them to merge into their surroundings. Although most are herbivores (plant-eaters,) some species can be partly predaceous, feeding on insect eggs and small, soft-bodied prey. In North America some species may have three or four generations in a year.

Order: Hemiptera – Family: Berytidae
NA species: 14 – World species: 180 – Body length: 1/4–1/3 ins

Pygmy Grasshoppers

Reasonably common in some areas, their habitat is moist woodlands and the margins of bogs and lakes. They eat grasses, mosses, and lichens. Unlike many species in this order, their courtship is silent. The male bows in front of the female and vibrates his wings. Members of this family do not stridulate (make the typical cricket sound) and have no hearing organs. Many species have gray or brown camouflage to match the mossy or stony ground where they live. There is still a great deal to be learned about their lifestyles. This could be a challenge for you to discover new facts.

Tetrix subulata
(Granulated Grouse Locust)

Order: Orthoptera
Family: Tetrigidae
NA species: 29
World species: 1,000
Body length: 1/4–3/4 ins

Alderflies

If you search for these in May and June, you will find them at rest on alder trees and similar waterside vegetation. They are lazy fliers, so you should be able to take a close look at one without disturbing it. A female may lay many hundreds of eggs in clusters on waterside plants. The young larvae crawl into the water and live there for nearly two years. When fully grown, the larvae crawl out of the water and pupate on the land.

Order: Megaloptera – Family: Sialidae
NA species: 23
World species: 75
Body length: 1/3–3/4 ins

Sialis lutaria

Mole Crickets

These generally reddish-brown insects show superb adaptations to subterranean life (underground.) The front legs are modified for digging. Their eyes are small and their wings are leathery, covering only half the abdomen. From the front they do look very like tiny moles. They live in sand or soil near streams, ponds, or lakes, and their burrows can go nearly 8 ins below ground. They build elaborate singing burrows with a special shape, which increases the volume of their song. On a still night they can be heard up to almost a mile away.

Order: Orthoptera – Family: Gryllotalpidae – NA species: 7
World species: 60 – Body length: 3/4–13/4 ins

Gryllotalpa gryllotalpa

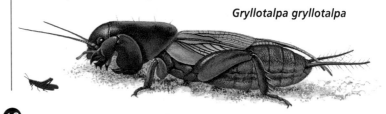

Shore Bugs

Saldula pallipes

As their name suggests, shore bugs are to be found around the margins of the seashore among seaweed, salt marshes, grasses, mosses, and low vegetation. These species can survive being submerged by the tide. Many, however, may be found by streams, ponds, ditches, and similar places. You will discover they are difficult to catch, as they hide away in holes and rock crevices. These bugs can run, jump and fly, or burrow into mud, where some spend part of their life cycle. As far as is known, all members of this family are predaceous (they hunt other creatures for food.)

Order: Hemiptera – Family: Saldidae
NA species: 76 – World species: 300 – Body length: 1/8–1/4 ins

Shore Flies

Psilopa compta

This family is to be found in many types of wetland, such as marshes, wet meadows, pool margins, lakes, rivers, and the seashore. Their larvae are either semi-aquatic or aquatic. They feed on sewage and carrion; some mine into meadow grasses, and others live in the stems of water plants. While most shore flies prefer fresh water, some can tolerate very salty water. You may find a cluster of them on the surface of a pool above the high tidemark. One unusual species can breed in pools of crude oil! A few of these flies have front legs like those of praying mantids (see page 32,) which they use to capture small insects.

Order: Diptera – Family: Ephydridae – NA species: 430
World species: 1,400 – Body length: 1/8–1/2 ins

Long-legged Flies

Dolichopus ungulatus

These flies will be found in wet habitats, such as marshy places, stream and lake margins, meadows, and woodland. A few species live on the seashore. The adults seize small insects, which they crush and chew before sucking up the juices. Look for them during the summer months. A great deal remains to be discovered about many of their larval ways of life. In the way that birds use parts of their body to signal to mates, these flies do the same. The males have hairy tufts and other "decoration" on their legs, which they show off to the females. When watching insects, always remember to keep your eyes open for aspects of their behavior.

Order: Diptera – Family: Dolichopodidae
NA species: 1,230 – World species: 5,500
Body length: Most under 1/8 ins

Striped Earwigs

Search for these nocturnal earwigs under debris, especially on seashores, mud flats, and the banks of rivers, but you will be lucky to find one because they are not very common. *Labidura riparia* (the Giant or Tawny Earwig, shown here) is the only one in this family to occur in North America. It prefers sandy habitats where it can dig deep tunnels in which to lay its eggs. Handle these earwigs gently because they will try to give you a pinch with their forceps. They might also discharge a smelly liquid and some species can fire it over a short distance.

Order: Dermaptera
Family: Labiduridae
NA species: 1
World species: 75
Body length: Up to 1 1/3 ins

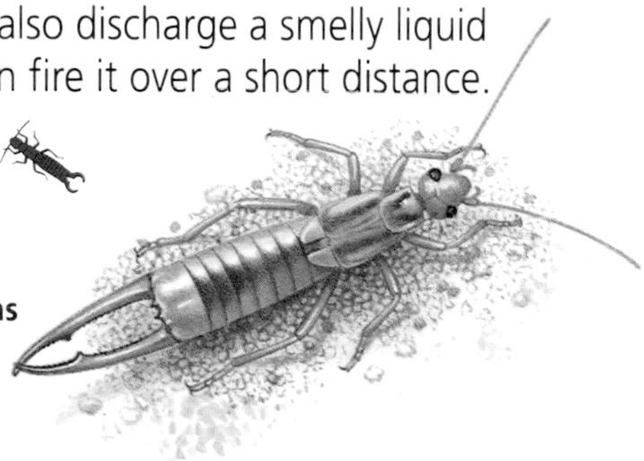

Water Measurers

This is a family of very slender, reddish to dark brown bugs. The genus *Hydrometra* is the most common in North America. They are found on quiet pools, marshes, swamps, stagnant and even brackish water. Their bodies and legs are well covered with a pile of fine hairs which repel water. They walk slowly on the surface near the water's edge. They skewer small insect larvae and other small water creatures on their tube-like mouthparts. The female lays her eggs singly and glues them to plants at the edge of the water, or to objects at water level. Search for them in June and July when new adults hatch from the eggs.

Order: Hemiptera
Family: Hydrometridae
NA species: 9
World species: 110
Body length: 1/2–3/4 ins

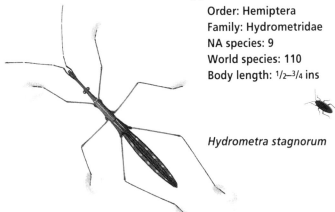

Hydrometra stagnorum

Backswimmers

Although they look a little like Water Boatmen (see opposite,) the backswimmers—as their name suggests—swim on their backs. Their long, hind legs are fringed with hairs and used as oars. Strong swimmers, they can leap into the air through the water's surface film and fly away. At rest they hang from the surface. They are underwater predators feeding on insects, small fish, tadpoles—and even fingers if given the chance! Males can make sounds to attract females by rasping their mouthparts on their front legs.

Order: Hemiptera
Family: Notonectidae
NA species: 35
World species: 300
Body length: 1/16–2/3 ins

Notonecta glauca

Water Striders

In this family, the feet and underside of the body have a dense covering of water-repellent hairs. This enables them literally to walk on the water's surface. Their legs also have ripple-sensitive hairs, so if you tap the water's surface, you will see them react. Look for these interesting insects on still or slow-running water. Most species have winged, short-winged, and wingless forms. The ones with wings can fly off to new sites and start new populations.

Order: Hemiptera
Family: Gerridae
NA species: 45
World species: 500
Body length: 1/16–1/4 ins

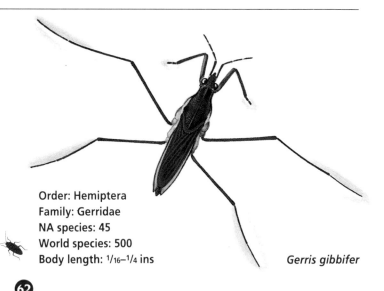

Gerris gibbifer

Water Boatmen

These are interesting insects that can swim rapidly and which carry their air supply as a bubble in a reservoir under their wings. This makes them buoyant, so they have to hang on to plants in order to remain in deeper water. Some species are predacious on other aquatic insects and even fish. Some species are unique among bugs because they can eat minute particles of solid food. All other bugs (Hemiptera) suck up liquid food. Corixids can fly well and are attracted to lights at night.

Order: Hemiptera
Family: Corixidae
NA species: 132
World species: 525
Body length: 1/8–1/2 ins

Glaenocorisa propinqua

Water Scorpions

Water scorpions lie in wait, hidden among vegetation, to ambush their prey. Their powerful front legs (known as raptorial legs) seize tadpoles, mosquito larvae, and most other small water creatures. Having seized their prey, they suck out the body juices. They thrust their long breathing tube out through the surface film to renew their air supply. Although they are fully winged, they seldom fly. You might be lucky and catch one if you push your pond net slowly through the water weeds in slow-moving or still water. However, be careful—they can give you a painful bite if handled carelessly.

Nepa cinerea

Order: Hemiptera
Family: Nepidae
NA species: 13
World species: 200
Body length: 1/2–13/4 ins

Predaceous Diving Beetles

Most diving beetles carry a supply of air enclosed in their wing cases. They renew it by projecting their tail end into the air. Their habitats vary from streams, ditches, canals, and lakes to ponds. If the habitat dries up, the beetles fly away to a new site. Both adults and larvae are predators on small fish, frogs, newts, snails, and many other kinds of water life. They suck out the body contents after injecting a digestive substance into their prey. When you go pond-dipping (see page 53,) you will almost certainly capture some.

Colymbetes fuscus

Order: Coleoptera – Family: Dytiscidae
NA species: 475 – World species: 3,500
Body length: 1/16–11/3 ins

Whirligig Beetles

Look for groups of these beetles on the surface of slow-moving water and ponds. If you gently tap the water surface, you will see them react by diving because their antennae are sensitive to ripples. Although adapted for water life, they can fly well. Their blue-black, highly polished, and streamlined upper body surfaces are waterproof. They use their middle and hind pairs of legs as oars and the front pair to seize mosquito larvae and dead insects floating on the surface.

Order: Coleoptera
Family: Gyrinidae
NA species: 58
World species: 750
Body length: 1/16–2/3 ins

Gyrinus minutus

Keeping Insects at Home

Have you ever thought of having your own insect zoo at home? Many kinds are easy to keep and it is great fun watching their behavior in close-up. However, you should only collect insects to observe them. Don't keep them more than 2–3 days, and always release them back into the habitat that you caught them in.

The rules for success are:
1 **Always handle insects very gently**—their legs and wings are often delicate.
2 **Keep the cage away from direct sunlight** and away from direct heat.
3 **Provide small air holes in the lid** or use fine netting. Insects breathe just as other animals do.
4 **Provide fresh food daily** and remove all uneaten food at the same time.
5 **Clean out the cages regularly**.

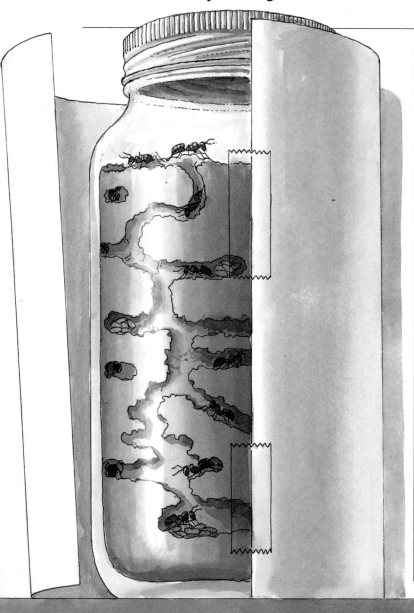

Insect cages

The best cages for insect watching are large jelly jars or preserving jars. If you are using the metal screw-on top as its lid, ask an adult to punch 6 to 8 small air holes into it. Or you can stretch a piece of fine material, like nylon, or muslin, over the top and attach it with a strong rubber band. Always put some leaves and a twig in the bottom of the jar so that the insects have some shelter. For a larger cage, like a fish tank, bend a wire coat hanger into a rough rectangle and fix the material onto it with staples. Weight the corners to prevent escapes.

Ant nest

You can easily make an ant home from a large glass jar. Partly fill it with soil and cover the outside with lightproof paper. Make sure the lid is antproof.
1 **Dig up an ant nest** in your backyard and try to find the biggest ant (a queen). Wear gloves as the worker ants will try to defend her.
2 **Put the queen in her new home** with as many workers as you can collect.
3 **Feed them every day** with a little sugar or honey sprinkled on the soil surface.
4 **In time they will excavate tunnels against the glass.** Remove the paper around the jar from time to time to see how they are doing.

What's inside?

Many different insects make galls. Why not collect and hatch them? In spring Gall Wasps (see page 40) lay their eggs on the buds of oak trees, which causes brown, marble-like galls to form. Inside the galls, the wasp larvae are growing, and in the fall, the adult wasps will eat their way out and fly off.

1 **Look for galls** on the ground in woods, on oaks, and many other plants and trees. Collect them in late summer and fall.
2 **Cut the twig or plant stem** so that it fits into a jelly jar.
3 **Cover the mouth of each jar** with a square of fabric and secure it with a rubber band.
4 **Put the jars in your garage**, tool shed, or on a balcony for the winter.
5 **In the spring, watch** for the tiny adult insects to emerge.

Mini vivarium

You can make a wonderful, ever-changing habitat in an old fish tank or large plastic candy jar. By adding stones, dead leaves, a clump of grass, and soil or sand, you can make a home for beetles and grasshoppers. A Long-horned Grasshopper (see page 43) will live well in a grassy tank with some branches for it to crawl about on. If you have two of them, you will most likely hear them singing after dark. Always release them after a few days.

Earwig nest

Earwigs (see page 10) will live quite comfortably in a plastic lunch box. Put moist—not wet—soil in the box with a couple of flat stones or a piece of bark for them to hide under. Add some ground litter in one corner. If you keep some earwigs between January and March, they may lay their eggs. They will need tiny pieces of raw meat and bits of lettuce, cucumber, or a slice of apple as food.

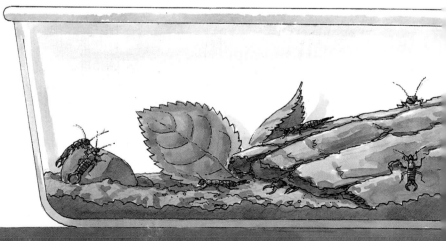

Pests & Parasites

These include insects that are pests of humans, their artifacts, buildings, livestock, and crops. A lot is known about parasites and the insect pests whose attacks cause commercial damage. But the enemies of the vast majority of insect species are, as yet, unknown.

Parasites are those insects that eat the living tissues of their host or prey. They do not necessarily kill their hosts, although many do. In general an insect parasite uses one host animal in or on which to carry out its complete development from egg to adult. The eggs may be laid on or in the host, and the hatching larvae feed on the host's body tissues or fluids. If they do this on the outside (like bed bugs,) they are called "ectoparasites." If they do it from within, they are called "endoparasites." Birds, as an example, have their own specialized insect parasites—fleas, louse flies, feather lice, etc.—while others live in their nests.

Houses have species that may "live on the premises," or may come in for a short stay through an open door or window. Food stores and warehouses attract a variety of insects that may become pests, simply because there are such quantities of the food they like to eat.

Most pests attack a specific crop—they can range from the annoying, like black fly on a rose tree, to life-threatening, like the plagues of locusts that sweep across Africa eating everything in their path. This picture shows nine species from this section; see how many can you identify?

Larder Beetle, Mealy Bug, House Fly (see page 15, Muscid Fly), Body Louse, Silverfish, Encyrtid Wasp, Ichneumon Wasp, Bean Weevil, Whitefly.

Parasites

Bird Lice

This family of tiny, wingless, parasitic lice have special claws adapted to hold on to their host's feathers. *Menopon gallinae* (the Shaft Louse, shown here) gives you a good idea of a typical family member. You are more likely to see their effect than to find the lice, unless you look very closely. The female attaches eggs singly to feathers by a waterproof, glue-like substance. The larvae then feed by scraping off the skin and feathers, which causes the bird to become bald in places and become unhealthy.

Order: Phthiraptera
Family: Menoponidae
NA species: 260
World species: 650
Body length:
$1/16$–$1/4$ **ins**

Human Lice

The eggs of this small family are commonly known as "nits." The adults have curved legs, each armed with a large claw for grasping hair. There is one species that lives on humans, but there are two distinct sub-species: the Body Louse (*Pediculus humanus corporis*) and the Head Louse (*Pediculus humanus capitis,* shown here.) The former lives in clothing, laying its eggs along the seams, but leaves to feed on human blood before hiding again. It carries typhus and other fevers. The Head Louse lives entirely in the hair and passes from host to host by headware, combs, brushes, and direct contact.

Order: Phthiraptera
Family: Pediculidae
NA species: 1
World species: 2
Body length:
$1/16$–$1/8$ **ins**

Mammal-chewing Lice

These small lice live in the micro-habitat provided by the hair or fur of their host mammal. Since they are always in very close contact with their host within a very small microhabitat, they do not need sight, so they have evolved as eyeless, or almost eyeless, insects. Some, like *Trichodectes canis* (the Dog Louse, shown here) are pests on domestic animals. This louse often transmits tapeworms from dog to dog. As they feed on skin, hair, fur, and blood, they cause great irritation to their hosts.

Order: Phthiraptera
Family: Trichodectidae
NA species: 137
World species: 350
Body length: $1/16$–$1/8$ **ins**

Common Fleas

The family of common fleas is ideally adapted to its habitats, which are the bodies of mammals and birds. The mouthparts are modified to pierce skin and suck blood. Fleas have narrow bodies, perfect for moving about between hairs. Their legs are long and strong, and they have a special spring built into the thorax which acts as an energy store, so they are great jumpers. The mechanism acts like a bow firing an arrow. *Ctenocephalides felis* (the Cat Flea, shown here) can high-jump around 100 times its own body length—about 13 ins. A single cat can support a very large population of fleas. Females lay their eggs on the ground and the larvae emerge. When they change to pupae, they can remain like that for years until a suitable animal comes along.

Order: Siphonaptera
Family: Pulicidae
NA species: 16 – **World species:** 200
Body length: $1/16$–$1/3$ **ins**

Flesh Flies

These flies live in a variety of habitats where they are able to feed on flower nectar, aphids' honeydew, or sap flowing from tree wounds. The adult females give birth to larvae and do not lay eggs. The food of species in the family varies: many feed on carrion (dead and rotting flesh.) Some are parasites on beetles, grasshoppers, and caterpillars of moths and butterflies, and some parasitize turtles and frogs. They look a little like blow flies (see page 14,) but are striped dull gray and black; they are never metallic. Some species are used to control insect pests.

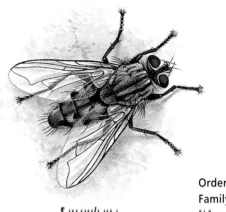

Sarcophaga haemorrhoidalis

Order: Diptera
Family: Sarcophagidae
NA species: 330
World species: 2,100
Body length: 1/16–3/4 ins

Bot & Warble Flies

The flies in this family are very heavy-bodied and look a little like honey or bumble bees. They often have hairy abdomens. *Oestris ovis* (the Sheep Bot Fly, shown here) gives you a good idea of their appearance. Their habitat tends to be close to their host species. In some species the males gather on hilltops for mating purposes.

Warble flies fasten their eggs very firmly to hairs on the legs of a cow, and the larvae burrow under the skin into the animal's back. When mature, they chew their way out and pupate in the soil, leaving a terrible sore.

Order: Diptera
Family: Oestridae
NA species: 41
World species: 160
Body length: 1/3–1 ins

Louse Flies

These strange-looking flies live as parasites, sucking blood from the bodies of birds or mammals, including deer, cattle, sheep, and horses. They have long, curved claws, which hold on to the fur or feathers of their active and moving habitat, and short antennae. As wings and eyes are not needed for their way of life, many species of the family have lost them. The female lays fully grown larvae which have grown inside her body feeding on special "milk glands." The mature larvae of *Melophagus ovinus* (the Sheep Ked, shown here) attach themselves to the sheep's wool by using a special glue before pupating.

Order: Diptera
Family: Hippoboscidae
NA species: 30
World species: 200
Body length: 1/16–1/2 ins

Parasites

Stylopids

These small parasites are seldom seen because of their way of life. The males look a bit like beetles. The females are grub-like and live on their hosts, especially andrenid bees, sand wasps, and the social wasps (see pages 19, 51, and 18). Their larvae crawl into flowers, where they wait to hitch a ride on a suitable host. Once aboard, they bore into the body and feed on its internal organs without killing it. After pupation in the host's body, the males fly away, but the females remain, with the tip of the body sticking out as shown here. The odor they give off attracts males to mate with them.

Order: Strepsiptera
Family: Stylopidae
NA species: 80
World species: 260
Body length: 1/16–1/8 ins

Stylops melittae

Bee Flies

You should look out for these hairy, bee-like flies on a sunny day. They can often be seen flying, hovering and sucking nectar from celandines and other early spring flowers. Do not worry about their bee-like buzzing—they have no sting. They lay eggs in the burrows of solitary bees and wasps; their larvae are parasitic on them, as well as beetles, moths, and other flies. The pupae have sharp teeth at one end, which break open the seal of the host cell so that the adult fly may escape.

Order: Diptera
Family: Bombyliidae
NA species: 800
World species: 5,000
Body length: 1/16–1 ins

Bombylius major

Tachinid Flies

Most of these look like bristly house flies, but some are very much larger, very hairy, and look rather like bees. They can be found in many habitats drinking nectar, tree sap, or honeydew (the secretion from aphids,) but they are hard to catch. Males of many species gather on hill tops waiting for females to fly near so that they may mate. All their larvae are parasitic upon other insects; the adults lay their eggs on or inside the host, which may be butterflies, beetles, bees, wasps, bugs, or flies. Parasitic flies are such efficient controllers of certain insect pests that many are used as biological control agents.

Voria ruralis

Order: Diptera – Family: Tachinidae
NA species: 1,280 – World species: 7,800
Body length: 1/16–1/2 ins

Fairyflies

This family of tiny wasps contains some of the smallest insects on Earth. The females lay their eggs inside the eggs of dragonflies, grasshoppers, butterflies and moths, beetles, and flies. One species, *Caraphractus cinctus* (shown here,) uses its wings to swim through the water to reach the submerged eggs of giant water beetles. They can remain under water for days at a time. Try to imagine how insects this small can search for and find the eggs they are going to parasitize.

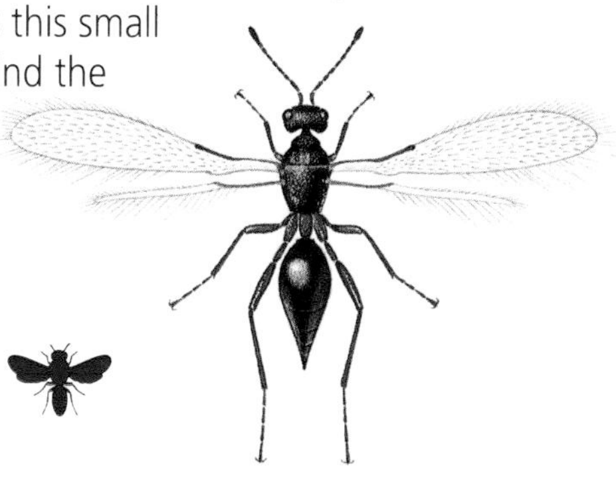

Order: Hymenoptera
Family: Mymaridae
NA species: 120
World species: 1,300
Body length: 1/16–1/8 ins

Braconid Wasps

Brown, reddish-brown or black, these wasps have quite slender bodies. They parasitize other insects; *Apanteles glomeratus* (shown here) searches out the larvae of the Cabbage White Butterfly to lay its eggs in them. The larvae then feed on the body of the host. Finally, some thirty or more larvae emerge and spin yellowish, silken cocoons on the outside of the host's body. Search for these "parasitized" caterpillars on cabbage leaves and other foliage, or on the walls of sheds and buildings. Leaving Cabbage Butterfly caterpillars in small tubes over the winter may also provide you with some parasitic wasps or flies. Many species from this family are used as biological control agents.

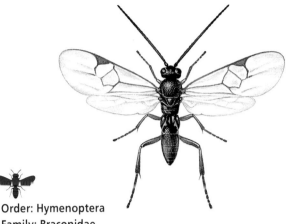

Order: Hymenoptera
Family: Braconidae
NA species: 2,000
World species: 15,000
Body length: 1/16–1/2 ins

Encyrtid Wasps

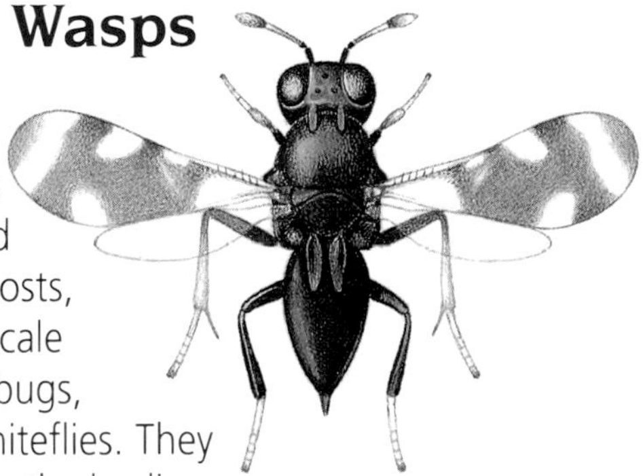

The majority of these wasps are to be found close to their hosts, which can be scale insects, mealy bugs, aphids, and whiteflies. They lay their eggs in the bodies of both immature and adult stages. Despite being so tiny, some of them lay eggs that divide repeatedly at a very early stage in their growth to produce between 10 and 2,000 larvae from a single egg. Others parasitize the larvae of braconid wasps which are already living as parasites in another larva. *Habrolepis dalmani* (shown here) is used to control a scale insect that damages oak trees, and other species have been used to control citrus pests.

Order: Hymenoptera – Family: Encyrtidae
NA species: 500 – World species: 3,000
Body length: 1/16–1/8 ins

Cuckoo Wasps

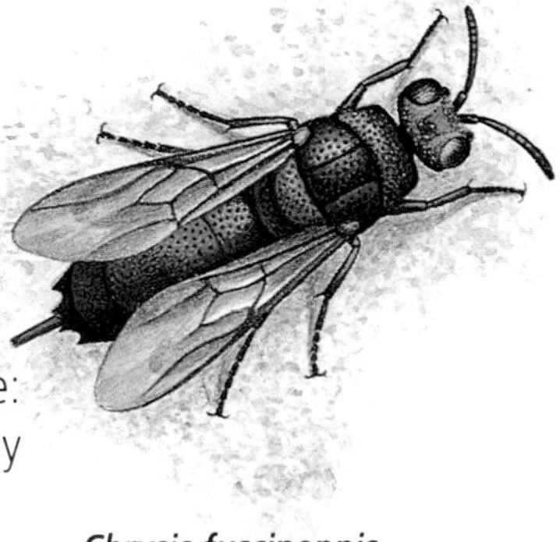

The body of the cuckoo wasp can be bright blue, green, red, copper, or mixed patterns, all with a shiny, metallic hue. This is how they get their other name: jewel wasps. On a hot, sunny day look along fences, sheltered walls, or banks where solitary bees and wasps may be living. They are parasites, searching for larval burrows in which to lay their eggs. However, they do not always eat their host, which is first paralyzed, but eat its food supply instead. Some species parasitize sawfly larvae (see page 19,) and a few eat praying mantis eggs (see page 32.)

Chrysis fuscipennis
These wasps often roll themselves into a ball as a protection against predators.

Order: Hymenoptera – Family: Chrysididae
NA species: 230 – World species: 3,000
Body length: 1/8–3/4 ins

Eulophid Wasps

These very tiny wasps are able to find many kinds of hidden larvae, like the leaf-blotch miner moths' larvae (see page 41.) They kill these larvae by laying eggs in their bodies. They are an important link in the chain of life because they help to control natural insect populations, such as those of moths, beetles, aphids, and scale insects. Today some species are bred and released into the environment to help control insect pests of larch and pine trees.

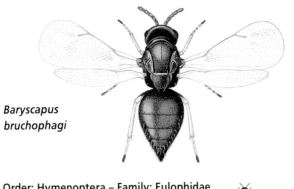

Baryscapus bruchophagi

Order: Hymenoptera – Family: Eulophidae
NA species: 510 – World species: 3,100
Body length: 1/16–1/4 ins

Pteromalid Wasps

All known pteromalid wasps are either black or a very metallic blue or green. Being parasitic, they are found everywhere that their host species live. A few form galls, while some are herbivores or hunt small insects, such as the larvae of the gall midge or the eggs of other insect species. The larvae of one world species destroys house flies and related insects, while another attacks fleas. These wasps are good examples of the useful work carried on by a tiny insect which very few of us have ever seen. There are still many undescribed species.

Order: Hymenoptera
Family: Pteromalidae
NA species: 400
World species: 3,200
Body length: 1/16–1/3 ins

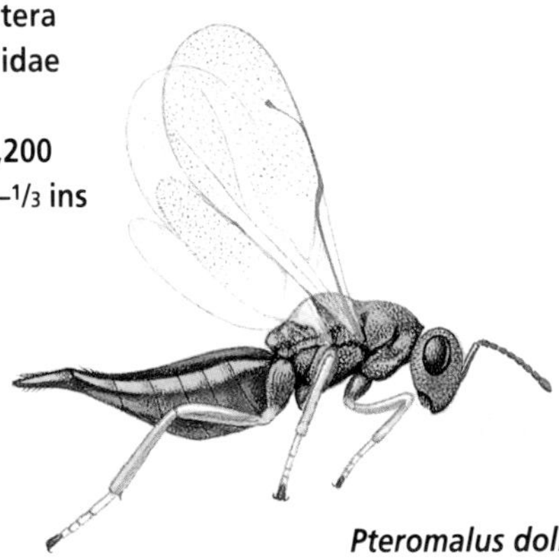

Pteromalus dolichurus

Ichneumon Wasps

If you see a long, narrow-bodied insect waving its antennae as it crawls about on a flat-topped flower, you may have found an ichneumon wasp. Most of the females have an ovipositor (long egg-laying tube.) The picture shows *Rhyssa persuasoria* using her antennae to scent out and find the larva of a horntail (see page 39,) which tunnels along tree trunks. When she finds one, she uses her ovipositor as a drill to bore down to the larva and place an egg on its body. It hatches and her larva then feeds on the body of the horntail larva. By sweeping your net among wild flowers, especially in damp habitats, you may find some of these wasps.

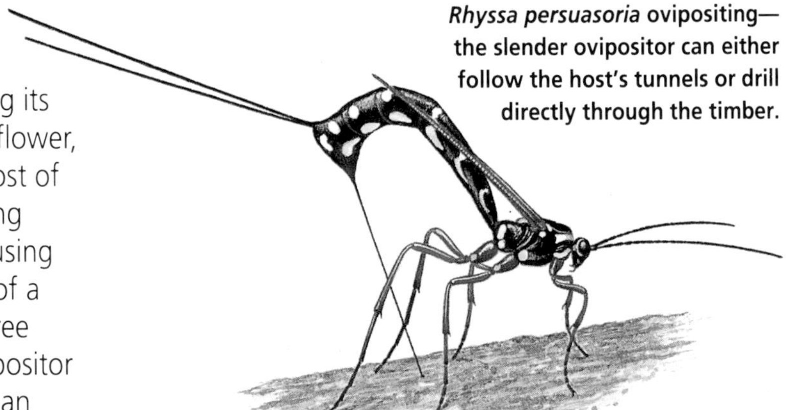

Rhyssa persuasoria ovipositing— the slender ovipositor can either follow the host's tunnels or drill directly through the timber.

Order: Hymenoptera – Family: Ichneumonidae
NA species: 3,350 – World species: 20,000
Body length: 1/8–1 2/3 ins

Platygastrid Wasps

Most species of platygastrid wasps lay eggs in the eggs or very young larvae of gall midges (see page 77,) mealybugs, or whiteflies (see page 75, both.) Species of *Inostemma* (shown here) have a forward-pointing "handle" which contains the ovipositor (egg-laying tube.) Their habitats are widespread, but are closely interlinked with the presence of whatever may be their host species. The life history of many species of these very small, shiny, black insects is still unknown.

Order: Hymenoptera – Family: Platygastridae
NA species: 200 – World species: 950
Body length:
1/16–1/8 ins

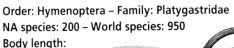

Scelionid Wasps

Like the platygastrid wasps, scelionid wasps have bent or elbowed antennae. Most of the adults are solitary and lay their eggs in the newly laid eggs of moths and butterflies. To be sure of such freshness these wasps have evolved the habit of clinging to the host insect until she lays her eggs. Some even lose their wings once they have found and boarded a suitable host insect. The species shown here, *Telenomus dalmanni*, parasitizes moth eggs.

Order: Hymenoptera
Family: Scelionidae
NA species: 280
World species: 1,250
Body length:
1/16–1/2 ins

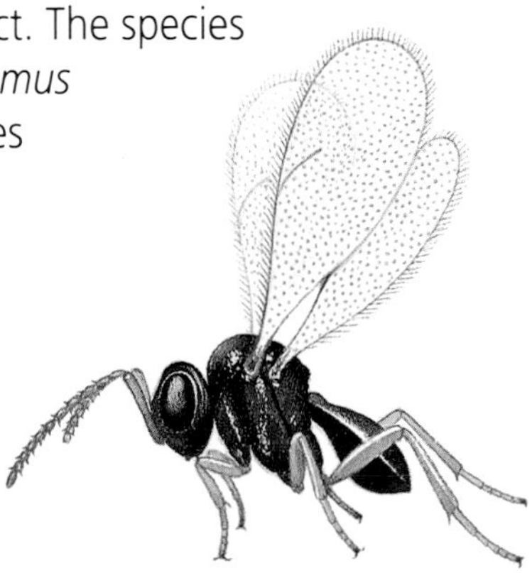

Torymid Wasps

As these wasps are very small; the best way to find them is to rear some galls (see page 65.) To sort them from other wasps that may also emerge, look for wasps with bright, shiny, metallic blue or green bodies. They will also have bent antennae and the ovipositor may be as long as, or even longer than, the rest of the body. While most species parasitize the occupants of galls, others parasitize caterpillars, the larvae of solitary bees and wasps, and some lay their eggs in the seeds of conifers, hawthorn, apple, and pear.

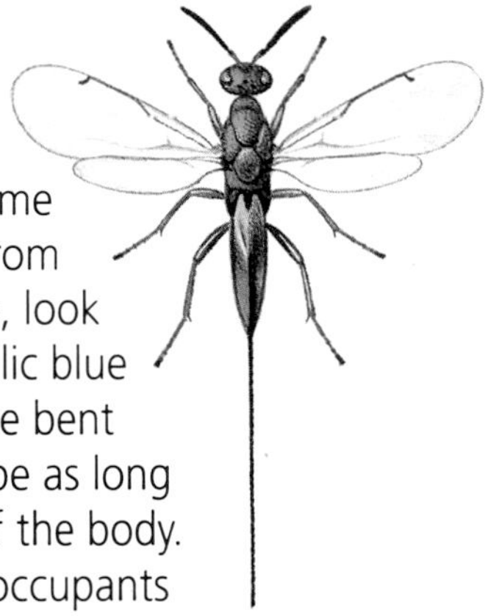

Torymus varians

Order: Hymenoptera – Family: Torymidae
NA species: 175 – World species: 1,500
Body length: 1/16–1/2 ins

Trichogrammatid Wasps

These lay their eggs into the eggs of a variety of other insects. To observe these tiny wasps you will need to collect insect eggs and wait to see what emerges. It is possible that one of them will be an undescribed species because the habits of so many of them are still unknown. The females of some species swim under water in search of the eggs of dragonflies and aquatic insects. Some species are very useful in controlling pest species.

Order: Hymenoptera
Family: Trichogrammatidae
NA species: 43
World species: 532
Body length:
1/32–1/16 ins

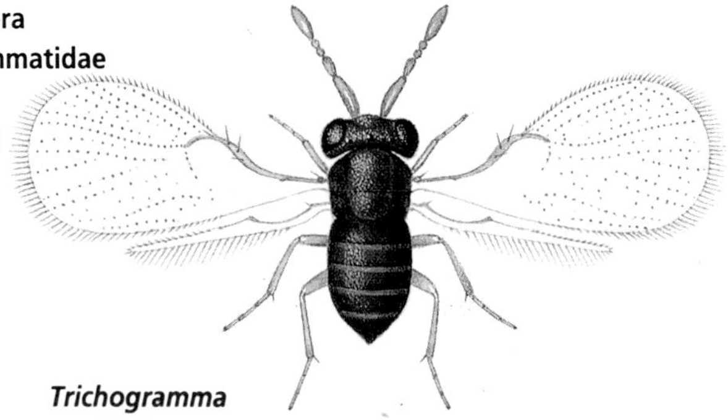

Trichogramma semblidis

House & Plant Pests

Silverfish & Firebrats

You may see some of these small, wingless, grayish or silver-scaled insects running about the kitchen or bathroom at night. The rear end has three tail-like filaments and they feed on flour, damp textiles, book bindings, and wallpaper paste. Most species live outdoors, so look for them under stones, in debris, and in ants' nests—they run for cover very fast, which often saves their lives. *Lepisma saccharina* (the Silverfish, shown here) prefers cool, damp microhabitats, while firebrats often stay near hot pipes and ovens.

Order: Thysanura – Family: Lepismatidae
NA species: 13
World species: 200
Body length:
1/3–3/4 ins

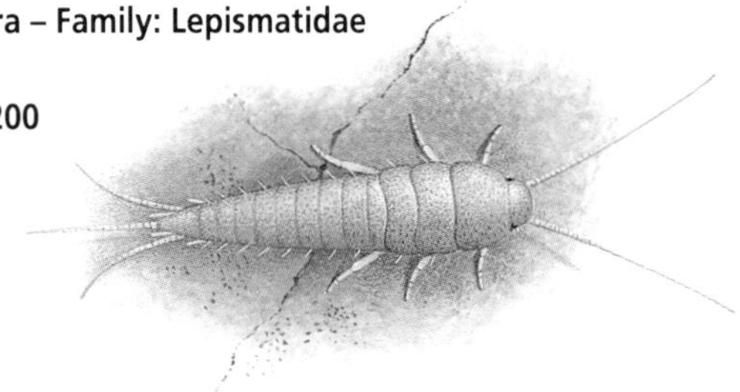

German Cockroaches

Members of this family look shiny and are generally brown or light brown in color. They have long, slender legs and long, thin antennae. Although they have wings, they seldom fly. A female lays an average of five egg cases and each one may contain about forty eggs. From each of these a young cockroach emerges, which looks exactly like a small adult. *Blattella germanica* (the German Cockroach, shown here) counts as a major household pest. They have an unpleasant smell, which will be obvious to you if they are around.

Order: Blattodea
Family: Blattellidae
NA species: 24
World species: 1,750
Body length: 1/3–1 ins

Clothes Moths

You may find some species from this family around rotting wood and fungi in a variety of habitats, but they are most common indoors where their larvae feed on woolen fabrics, fur, and textiles. The female *Tineola bisselliella* (Webbing Clothes Moth, shown here) lays about 100 eggs in the folds of clothing. When the larvae emerge, they spin a tube made from the gnawed material as a protection against drying out. With the increase of man-made fibers and insect repellents, many of the family are becoming scarcer, though some remain serious pests, particularly in museums.

Order: Lepidoptera
Family: Tineidae
NA species: 180
World species: 2,500
Body length:
1/3–3/4 ins

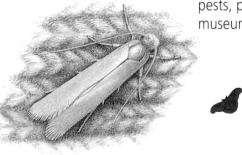

Bed Bugs

These blood-sucking bugs have oval, flattened bodies, and some have a covering of silky hairs. They are parasitic on humans, other mammals, and birds. Where humans live in crowded and insanitary places, they are common. At night they suck the blood of their hosts and return to their hiding places. In a single meal an adult *Cimex lectularius* (Bed Bug, shown here) can suck up seven times its own weight of blood. The nymphs take 6–26 weeks to develop—they need a blood meal at each of the five molts during their growth.

Order: Hemiptera
Family: Cimicidae
NA species: 14
World species: 90
Body length: 1/16–1/4 ins

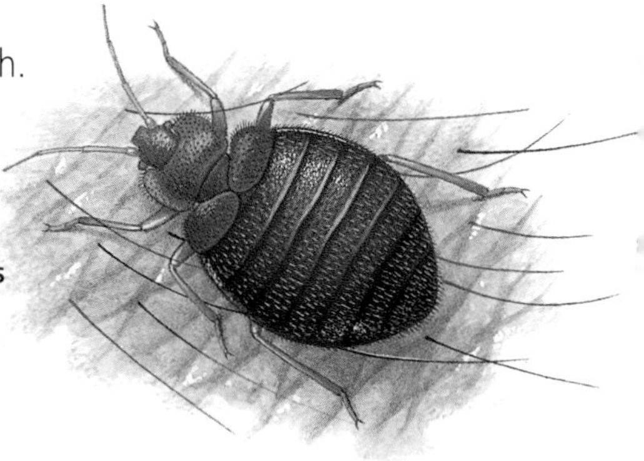

Wax & Tortoise Scale Insects

In general, scale insects are oval and flattened and have a hard waxy or smooth body. Most of the females remain fixed in one place on a plant and do not look like insects at all. *Coccus hesperidum* (shown here) is a pest of greenhouse crops and citrus trees. A single female may produce hundreds of millions of eggs in one year. From these emerge nymphs, called "crawlers," who move away from their mother before pushing their "beaks" into the plant to suck sap. Many nymphs produce wax filaments that allow them to lift off on the wind and travel great distances.

Order: Hemiptera – Family: Coccidae
NA Species: 92 – World species: 1,250 – Body length: 1/16–1/2 ins

Mealy Bugs

Unlike other scale insects, members of this family have legs at all stages in their life cycle. The females are wingless and are covered in a mealy or waxy white coating. The males look more like proper insects with a pair of wings, but their mouthparts are undeveloped, so they cannot feed. All mealy bug species are sap suckers. The females of some species lay eggs, but others give birth to live nymphs. Mealy bugs are found on a variety of host plants; each species tends to keep to a particular type of plant.

Order: Hemiptera
Family: Pseudococcidae
NA species: 280
World species: 2,000
Body length: 1/16–1/8 ins

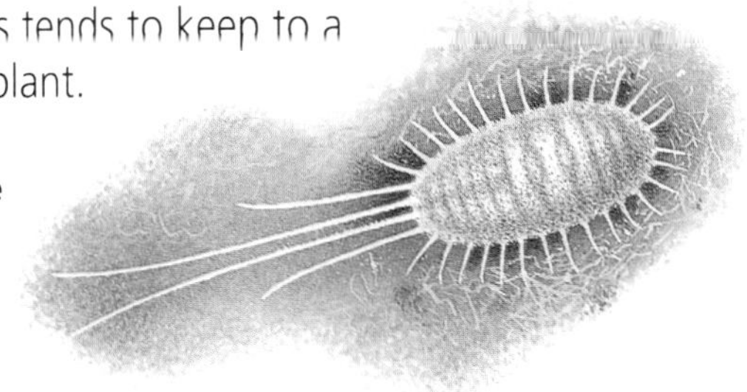

Pseudococcus adonidum

Whiteflies

If your parents have a greenhouse, or simply keep a few house plants at home, you may have heard about the whitefly problem. The females of *Trialeurodes vaporariorum* (the Greenhouse Whitefly, shown here) lay eggs on the underside of leaves. The nymphs suck the plant sap and excrete honeydew. In turn, this sugary fluid attracts a fungus (*Botrytis*) which covers the plant in black smudges. A whitefly population explosion can be controlled by using a small parasitic wasp called *Encarsia formosa*. This is cheaper and safer than using chemicals.

Order: Hemiptera
Family: Aleyrodidae
NA species: 100
World species: 1,200
Body length: 1/16–1/8 ins

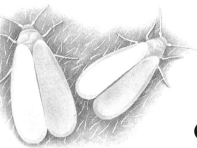

Leaf-footed Bugs

The males of some species have strong hind legs armed with spines. These are used in territorial fighting for access to females. All species are herbivorous (plant-eating) and defend themselves by spraying a pungent, unpleasant fluid at their enemies. Some species may be found feeding on St. Johnswort, grasses, and other plants. In North America a few species damage members of the Gourd family—including melons, marrows, and pumpkins.

Order: Hemiptera
Family: Coreidae
NA species: 120
World species: 2,000
Body length: 1/3–1 1/2 ins

Coriomeris scabricornis

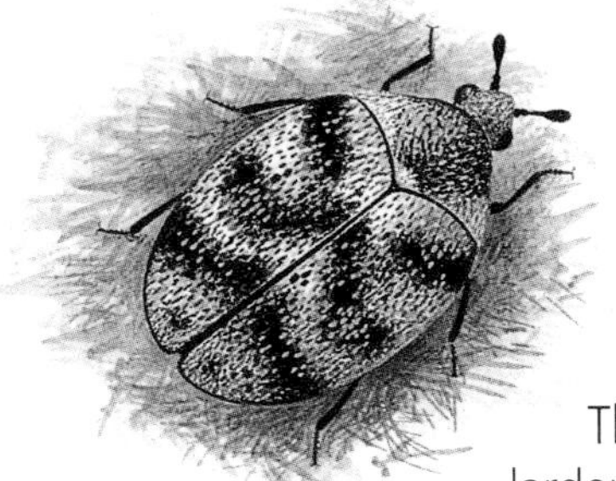

House & Plant Pests

Dermestid Beetles

This family of small beetles can be found in a huge variety of indoor and outdoor habitats. They are also known as skin, larder, and museum beetles. Their food, when larvae, is mainly the dried remains of plants or animals, including hair and feathers. Others thrive on a diet of carpets, fur, spices, or dried milk. Many museum collections of organic (plant- or animal-based) materials have been destroyed by *Anthrenus verbasci* (the Museum Beetle, shown here.) The adults mostly eat pollen from flowers.

Order: Coleoptera – Family: Dermestidae
NA species: 130 – World species: 800
Body length: 1/16–1/2 ins

Scarab Beetles & their relatives

The sacred scarabs of ancient Egypt are part of this family. Their habitat is extremely varied, but includes fungi, flowers, dung, bark and the nests of ants, termites, and vertebrates. There are many sub-families with common names like dung beetles, cockchafers, skin beetles, rose chafers, rhinoceros, and hercules beetles. It is one of the largest families of beetles with 1,400 species. In early summer you may see and hear a June beetle or June bug flying toward a lighted window on a warm night.

Serica brunnea

Order: Coleoptera
Family: Scarabaeidae
NA species: 1,400
World species: 20,000
Body length: 1/16–6 ins

Pea & Bean Weevils

These pests of stored products lay their eggs on seeds and these produce whitish, grub-like larvae that burrow into peas and beans. Many larvae may develop inside a single seed, thus destroying it. When fully grown, they pupate near the surface and on emergence they chew their way out. This action leaves a small, round hole—a sure sign that the culprit was a pea or bean weevil. Some species attack crops in the field, like *Callosobruchus maculatus* (the Cowpea Weevil, shown here.)

Order: Coleoptera
Family: Bruchidae
NA species: 135 – World species: 1,300
Body length: 1/16–3/4 ins

Click Beetles

These beetles have the ability to click loudly and throw themselves into the air when lying on their backs. The very loud click and the sudden movement will frighten any predator, while moving the beetle out of harm's way. You may find one in your beating tray, especially from oak trees. They are also found on the ground under leaf litter and in decaying wood. The larvae are called wireworms because they are thin and tough-bodied. They are found under bark, in rotten wood, and in soil.

Order: Coleoptera   *Agriotes lineatus*
Family: Elateridae
NA species: 890
World species: 8,500
Body length: 1/16–2 1/3 ins

Gall Midges

Many members of this family lay eggs in the leaves of plants and so make galls form in the daisy, grass, and willow families. They can be found anywhere that their host plants grow. Some species of gall midges produce larvae that are parasitic on small insect mites, while others are predators. A few species live in fungi, and some even live in galls made by other insects.

Mayetiola destructor (the Hessian Fly)—the larva is a pest on wheat, rye, and barley.

Order: Diptera – Family: Cecidomyiidae
NA species: 1,060 – World species: 4,600
Body length: $^1/_{16}$–$^1/_3$ ins

Pomace Flies

Tiny flies of this family, also known as Lesser Fruit Flies, have been studied in more detail than any other animal. They are of immense help in the study of genetics because they are small, can be easily bred on artificial foods, and reproduce very fast. In the wild they are found near rotting fruit, and elsewhere in food and drink processing factories. Search around decaying, fallen apples to find tiny flies with red eyes that look like the one shown here (*Drosophilia funebris*.)

Order: Diptera
Family: Drosophilidae
NA species: 117
World species: 2,900
Body length: $^1/_{16}$–$^1/_4$ ins

Clear-winged Moths

These moths are truly amazing. They mimic social wasps, bees, or ichneumon wasps, and resemble them very closely in body shape and color. To increase the illusion, even their wings are almost free of scales. *Sesia apiformis* (the Hornet Clearwing Moth, shown here) mimics a hornet. They complete the mimicry by buzzing, and some species even pretend to sting, so if you do see one, look carefully and make sure it really is a clearwing. They can be seen around flowers in a variety of habitats.

Order: Lepidoptera
Family: Sesiidae
NA species: 120 – World species: 1,000
Wingspan: $^1/_2$–$1^1/_2$ ins

Gelechiid Moths

These small to tiny moths form one of the largest moth families. The caterpillars of some species protect themselves by rolling leaves into a tube fastened with their silk. Others spin shelters of silk in the leaves, shoots, or flower heads of host plants. By looking closely at a number of oak leaves in late summer, you should be able to find some of these leaf-rollers. Many species are pests on crops, such as potatoes, tomatoes, strawberries, and soft fruit.

Order: Lepidoptera
Family: Gelechiidae
NA species: 635
World species: 4,200
Wingspan: $^1/_4$–1 ins

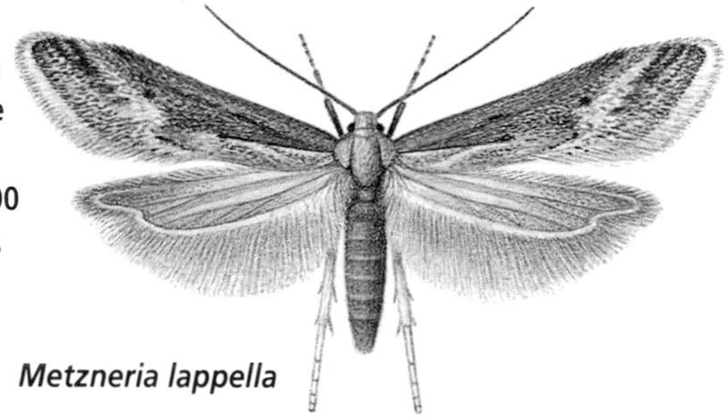

Metzneria lappella

Find Out Some More

Useful Organizations

In addition to the national groups listed below, there are hundreds of local societies and groups studying just one family of insects. Check with your teacher, or with your nearest natural history museum, wildlife refuge, or local public library for information on them.

The **Young Entomologist's Society** publishes a quarterly magazine containing general articles about insects which are of interest to the beginner. Write to: Young Entomologist's Society, 1915 Peggy Place, Lansing, Michigan 48910.

If you are interested in butterflies and moths, **The Lepodopterist's Society** publishes a journal and a newsletter. Write to: The Lepodopterist's Society, c/o Dr. William Winter, 257 Common Street, Dedham, Massachusetts 02026–4020.

The **Dragonfly Society of America** focuses on these spectacular insects. Write to: The Dragonfly Society of America, 469 Crailhope Road, Center, Kentucky 42214.

The **American Entomological Society** is for professional entomologists and serious amateurs. It publishes *Entomological News*. Write to: American Entomological Society, Academy of Natural Sciences of Philadelphia, 1900 Race Street, Philadelphia, Pennsylvania 19103.

The **Xerces Society** is another national society for butterfly enthusiasts. Write to: Xerces Society, c/o Melody Allen, 10 Southwest Ash Street, Portland, Oregon 97204.

Many of the preserves owned by the **Nature Conservancy** and its chapters, conserve unique and threatened habitats for insects. Write to: Nature Conservancy, Suite 800, 1800 North Kent Street, Arlington, Virginia 22209.

In Canada, the **Canadian Nature Foundation** is a good starting point. Write to: Canadian Nature Foundation, 453 Sussex Drive, Ottawa, Ontario K1N 6Z4.

Places To Visit

Insects can be found virtually everywhere, from wild prairies to city sidewalks. Here is a selection of different regional habitats where a variety of insects can be found:

Big Cypress National Reserve, Ochopee, Florida: This has a wide variety of habitats, including sawgrass marshes, hardwood hammocks, and mangrove stands. It hosts many subtropical insects not found in the rest of the U.S.

Shenandoah National Park, Luray, Virginia: Many insects typical of the Appalachian oak forests are common here. If you see a large area of dead trees, they are likely to be the work of gypsy moths, a pest imported from Europe.

Black Kettle National Grassland, Cheyenne, Oklahoma: Here there are large lakes surrounded by tall grass prairie. They hold many grassland species of butterflies, plus dragonflies, and other insects.

Coronado National Forest, Arizona: More than 1.7 million acres, ranging from desert to mountains, makes this an ideal place to search for southwestern insects.

Death Valley National Monument, Death Valley, California: The hottest point in North America and the lowest spot in the Western Hemisphere, Death Valley looks barren, but it supports many forms of life, including desert insects.

North Cascades National Park, Sedro Woolley, Washington: High in the Cascade Mountains, this park has deep forests and mountain (alpine) meadows full of wild flowers. While there are not as many different insects here, it is a good place to look for northern species.

There are also many preserves and refuges in every state—check with your teacher, or with your nearest natural history museum, wildlife refuge, or local public library for information on them.

Index & Glossary

To find the name of an insect in this index, search under its main name. So, to look up **True Cricket**; look under **Cricket**, not under **True**. The names of insect families are shown in **bold** type.

A

abdomen the third section of an insect's body. It carries the *ovipositor* and the sting, (see opposite the title page)
Alderflies, 60
Antlions, 49
Ants, 11
   Velvet, 51
Aphids, 16
Archaeognatha, 10

B

Blattodea, 10, 74
Backswimmers, 62
Barklice, Common, 42
   Narrow, 40
Bees, Andrenid, 19
   Carpenter, 50
   Cuckoo, 50
   Digger, 50
   Halictid, 19
   Honey, 19
   Leaf-cutter, 18
   Mason, 18
   Mining, 19
   Plasterer, 18
   Sweat, 19
   Yellow-faced, 18
Beetles, Bark, 38

Blister, 49
Burying, 12
Carrion, 12
Checkered, 13
Click, 76
Darkling, 50
Death-watch, 38
Dermestid, 76
Earth-boring Dung, 27
Engraver, 38
Ground, 12
Ladybug, 44
Leaf, 13
Long-horned, 42
Metallic Wood-boring, 38
Oil, 49
Pleasing Fungus, 44

Predacious Diving, 63
Rove, 12
Sap, 13
Scarab, 76
Snout, 13
Soldier, 27
Stag, 44
Tiger, 49
Tumbling Flower, 27
Whirligig, 63
Boatmen, Water, 63
Bristletails, Jumping, 10
Bugs, Assassin, 16
   Bed, 74
   Damsel, 31
   Lace, 42
   Leaf-footed, 75
   Mealy, 75

   Minute Pirate, 17
   Plant, 17
   Scentless Plant, 30
   Seed, 31
   Shore, 61
   Spittle, 30
   Stilt, 60
   Stink, 17
   Thread-legged, 16
Bumblebees, 19
Butterflies, Arctic, 45
   Atlas, 45
   Brush Footed, 21
   Emperor, 45
   Gossamer-winged, 20
   Milkweed, 33
   Moon, 45
   Nymph, 45
   Orange-tip, 22
   Royal, 45
   Satyr, 45
   Skipper, 33
   Sulfur, 22
   Swallowtail, 33
   White, 22

C

Caddisflies, Large, 59
   Micro, 59
   Northern, 59
carnivorous any animal that eats meat, 58
caterpillars, tent, 43
Cicadas, 40
Cockroaches, 10
Cockroaches, German, 74
Coleoptera, 12, 13, 27, 38, 41, 42, 44, 49, 50, 63, 76

Useful Books

All Upon a Sidewalk, Jean Craighead George (E.P. Dutton). A fascinating exploration of ants.
Golden Guide to Moths and Butterflies, Robert T. Mitchell & Herbert S. Zim (Golden Press).
A Guide to Observing Insect Lives, Donald Stokes (Little, Brown & Co.).
Insect & Spider Collections of the World, R.H. Arnett & A. Samuelson (Flora & Fauna Publications, Gainesville, Florida). Find out where your nearest collection of insects is housed.
Insects of the Northern Hemisphere, George C. McGavin (Smithmark). Spiral-bound pocket guide.
1001 Questions Answered About Insects, Alexander & Elsies Klots (Dodd, Mead Co.).
Peterson First Guide: Caterpillars, Amy Bartlett Wright (Houghton Mifflin Co.).
The World of Dragonflies & Damselflies, Ross E. Hutchins (Dodd, Mead Co.).

Index & Glossary

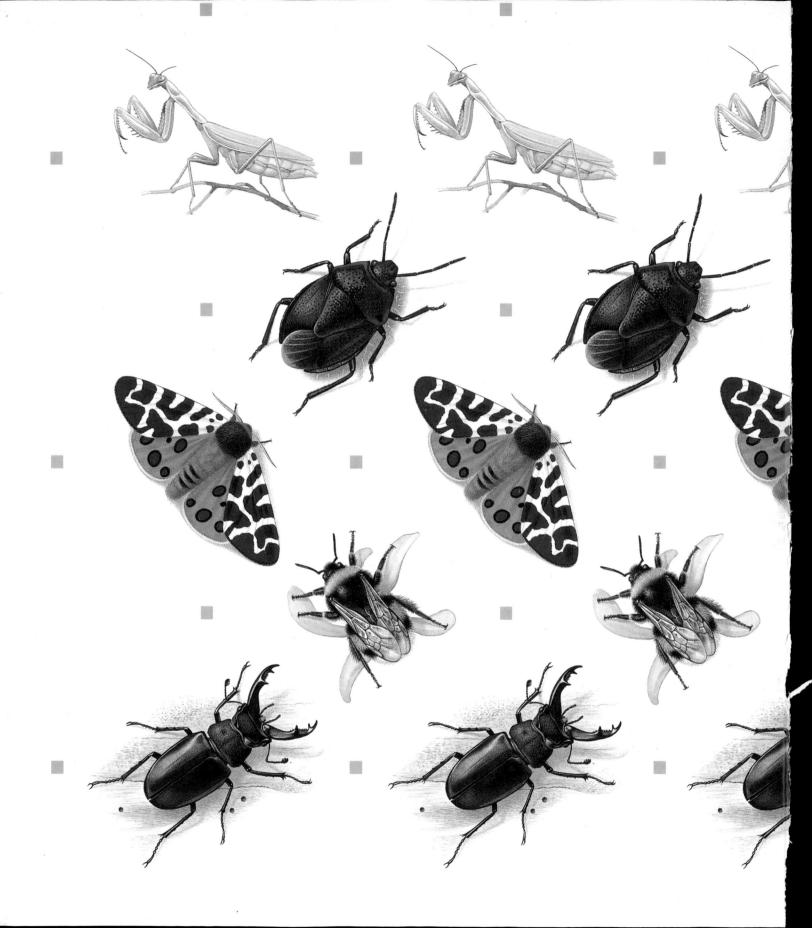